To Mom on her
birthday 1968
From
Denise & Sherie

The Vision

OR

The Degrees of Glory

(Doc. and Cov. Section 76)

Being a compilation of rare and invaluable writings by Authorities of the Church of Jesus Christ of Latter-day Saints, as well as quotations from Eminent Historians, Philosophers, Catholic Fathers and Protestant leaders.

on

THE DOCTRINE OF SALVATION FOR THE LIVING AND THE DEAD

N. B. LUNDWALL
Compiler

BOOKCRAFT PUBLISHING CO.
SALT LAKE CITY, UTAH

AUTHENTICITY OF THIS BOOK

Before the publication of this book, the manuscript was submitted to the late Elder Melvin J. Ballard and also to the Office of the First Presidency and to members of the Church Historian's Office, and upon recommendation two or three items were omitted. In taking up the matter of having a formal approval, one of the Apostles stated to the Compiler that nothing that he could say would add to the book as it was a very choice compilation and that the authorities quoted was approval enough. Another Apostle stated: "That is what the Saints need;" another prominent authority stated: "That book should be in every home." In going over the list of authorities quoted: viz., the Lord Jesus Christ, the Saviour of the world, the Prophet Joseph, Brigham Young, Heber C. Kimball, John Taylor, Wilford Woodruff, Lorenzo Snow, Joseph F. Smith, Parley P. Pratt, Orson Pratt, and the other prominent authorities—which one of these should have his views questioned? If the views of the authorities quoted are not sound, where can sound views be obtained? The statement of President Brigham Young in the INTRODUCTION to this book is respectfully referred to those who do not think for themselves. No one has a monopoly on truth. It is felt that this book contains gems of truth worthy of the consideration of any and all persons.

INTRODUCTION

It is hoped that he who reads this book may do so with an unbiased and open mind. Mankind are universally prejudiced to a greater or less degree, and hesitate to accept new spiritual truths, especially so if its source is unpopular, "whether found on heathen or Christian ground." This is especially so with respect to what is generally called "Mormonism," which is truly the Gospel of Jesus Christ, the power of God unto salvation.

Words written or spoken under the influence of the Spirit of God will sink deeply into the heart of anyone who is hungering and thirsting after righteousness. This will be true of the writings in this book. It is desired that the reader of this compilation of rare and precious material may comprehend the dignity, majesty, justice and benevolence of it all, and that conviction of its truth will follow its reading to the extent that he may attain to the inexpressibly great goal described in the following statement by President Brigham Young—a goal attainable only by those who are courageously and valiantly battling for the triumph of truth in the earth.

"I wish to notice this. We read in the Bible, that there is one glory of the sun, another glory of the moon, and another glory of the stars. In the Book of Doctrine and Covenants, these glories are called telestial, terrestrial, and celestial, which is the highest. These are worlds, different departments, or mansions, in our Father's house. Now those men, or those women, who know no more about the power of God, and the influences of the Holy Spirit, than to be led entirely by another person, suspending their own understanding, and pinning their faith upon another's sleeve, will never be capable of entering into celestial glory, to be crowned as they anticipate; they will never be capable of becoming Gods. They cannot rule themselves to say nothing of ruling others, but they must be dictated to in every trifle, like a child. They cannot control themselves in the least, but James, Peter, or somebody else must control them. They never can become Gods, nor be crowned as rulers with glory, immortality, and eternal lives. They never can hold sceptres of glory, majesty, and power in the celestial kingdom. Who will? Those who are valiant and inspired with the true independence of heaven, who will go forth boldly in the service of their God, leaving others to do as they please, determined to do right, though all mankind besides should take the opposite course. Will this apply to any of you? Your own hearts can answer."

Pres. Brigham Young, Journal of Discourses, Vol. 1, p. 312.

TABLE OF CONTENTS

TABLE OF CONTENTS—Continued

MANY SIMILAR TESTIMONIALS ARE AVAILABLE

"Orson Pratt was a man of unusual intellectual gifts. I know of none who has succeeded better in setting forth the claims as well as the philosophy of the Church of Jesus Christ of Latter-day Saints. His writings are not nearly as well known as they should be by the members of the Church and the public generally. I am very glad that you have collected some of the precious writings of Orson Pratt and made them into a volume of acceptable size for the readers of this day. I am sure that those who purchase the volume will find much enjoyment in the perusal of its pages.

JOHN A. WIDTSOE."

* * *

"To the earnest student desiring to understand life, the universe around us, and the planet on which we live, I heartily recommend 'WONDERS OF THE UNIVERSE.' I consider this book to be one of the finest in my library. Text books treating subjects dealt with in this work are mostly far beyond the layman. The simplicity of the language in the 'WONDERS OF THE UNIVERSE' is within the scope of the average earnest student desiring to broaden his education and general knowledge.

"It is a book I turn to time and again for real food for thought, and I assure you I value my copy very highly.

EDWIN BUTTERWORTH."

* * *

"We prize our copy of 'THE VISION' and consider its value second only to the Standard Works of the Church in teaching the three degrees of glory. We consider this book one of the very best books; it is interesting, instructive and inspiring. We thank you for making it possible for us to enjoy it.

MR. AND MRS. J. H. SAXTON, 366 Quince St., Salt Lake City."

* * *

"I am writing to you to let you know how I have enjoyed reading your recent publication, THE VISION. I think it is one of the finest books I have read in years. There isn't a single article in it that isn't worth the entire cost of the book.

"I am on my 29th consecutive year as a Sunday School teacher and find invaluable as a text book on the principles of the gospel. In my mind you have done the Church and the members of the Church a distinct favor by publishing this book. It should be in every L. D. S. home.

JOSEPH E. WOOD, Senior President of the 137th Quorum of Seventy, Salt Lake City."

* * *

"While on my sick bed at the L. D. S. Hospital, I had the rare privilege of reading THE VISION, your book of compilations of rare and invaluable writings of sermons delivered by the Prophet Joseph Smith and other authorities since the 76th Section of the Doctrine and Covenants was given.

"Having buried my father and three stalwart sons within the past ten months, this book was the key to spiritual understanding of eternal life and the most comforting testimony of the reason for loved ones departing.

"I am indeed grateful to you and our Heavenly Father for the light manifested in this compilation. Money could not buy my copy if I knew it would not have further publishing after this edition.

"God bless you in your future efforts to help man.

Sincerely,
GRANT S. WOODWARD, Salt Lake City."

* * *

"Your book was received and we have read it through and we both think it is marvelous. Keep the good work going. We feel that the information in this book is worth its weight in gold. We would surely dread to part with ours. We cannot say too much in praise of THE VISION and the splendid teachings of the Prophet Joseph.

ELNORA AND ZEKE JOHNSON, Blanding, Utah."

THE OCCASION OR BACKGROUND FOR RECEIVING "THE VISION"

By Joseph the Prophet

"Upon my return from Amherst conference, I resumed the translation of the Scriptures. From sundry revelations which had been received, it was apparent that many important points touching the salvation of man had been taken from the Bible, or lost before it was compiled. It appeared self-evident from what truths were left, that if God rewarded every one according to the deeds done in the body the term "Heaven" as intended for the Saints' eternal home, must include more kingdoms than one. Accordingly, on the 16th day of February, 1832, while translating St. John's Gospel, myself and Elder Ridgon saw the following vision:

ॐ

"THE VISION," OR THE 76TH SECTION OF DOCTRINE AND COVENANTS

Hear, O ye heavens, and give ear, O earth, and rejoice ye inhabitants thereof, for the Lord is God, and beside him there is no Saviour:

Great is his wisdom, marvelous are his ways and the extent of his doings none can find out;

His purposes fail not, neither are there any who can stay his hand;

From eternity to eternity he is the same, and his years never fail.

For thus saith the Lord, I, the Lord, am merciful and gracious unto those who fear me, and delight to honor those who serve me in righteousness and in truth unto the end;

Great shall be their reward and eternal shall be their glory;

And to them will I reveal all mysteries, yea, all the hidden

[1]

mysteries of my kingdom from days of old, and for ages to come will I make known unto them the good pleasure of my will concerning all things pertaining to my kingdom;

Yea, even the wonders of eternity shall they know, and things to come will I show them, even the things of many generations;

And their wisdom shall be great, and their understanding reach to heaven; and before them the wisdom of the wise shall perish, and the understanding of the prudent shall come to naught;

For by my Spirit will I enlighten them, and by my power will I make known unto them the secrets of my will; yea, even those things which eye has not seen, nor ear heard, nor yet entered into the heart of man.

We, Joseph Smith, jun., and Sidney Rigdon, being in the Spirit on the sixteenth of February, in the year of our Lord, one thousand eight hundred and thirty-two,

By the power of the Spirit, our eyes were opened and our understandings were enlightened, so as to see and understand the things of God—

Even those things which were from the beginning before the world was, which were ordained of the Father, through his Only Begotten Son, who was in the bosom of the Father, even from the beginning.

Of whom we bear record, and the record which we bear is the fullness of the gospel of Jesus Christ, who is the Son, whom we saw and with whom we conversed in the heavenly vision;

For while we were doing the work of translation, which the Lord had appointed unto us, we came to the twenty-ninth verse of the fifth chapter of John, which was given unto us as follows:

Speaking of the resurrection of the dead, concerning those who shall hear the voice of the Son of Man, and shall come forth;

They who have done good in the resurrection of the just, and they who have done evil in the resurrection of the unjust.

Now this caused us to marvel, for it was given unto us of the Spirit;

THE DEGREES OF GLORY

And while we meditated upon these things, the Lord touched the eyes of our understandings and they were opened, and the glory of the Lord shone round about;

And we beheld the glory of the Son, on the right hand of the Father, and received of his fullness;

And saw the holy angels, and they who are sanctified, before his throne, worshiping God, and the Lamb, who worship him for ever and ever.

And now, after the many testimonies which have been given of him, this is the testimony last of all, which we give of him, that he lives;

For we saw him, even on the right hand of God; and we heard the voice bearing record that he is the Only Begotten of the Father—

That by him, and through him, and of him, the worlds are and were created, and the inhabitants thereof are begotten sons and daughters unto God.

And this we saw also, and bear record, that an angel of God who was in authority in the presence of God, who rebelled against the Only Begotten Son, whom the Father loved, and who was in the bosom of the Father—was thrust down from the presence of God and the Son.

And was called Perdition, for the heavens wept over him— he was Lucifer, a son of the morning.

And we beheld, and lo, he is fallen! is fallen! even a son of the morning.

And while we were yet in the Spirit, the Lord commanded us that we should write the vision, for we beheld Satan, that old serpent—even the devil—who rebelled against God, and sought to take the kingdom of our God, and his Christ.

Wherefore he maketh war with the saints of God, and encompasses them round about.

And we saw a vision of the sufferings of those with whom he made war and overcame, for thus came the voice of the Lord unto us.

Thus saith the Lord, concerning all those who know my power, and have been made partakers thereof, and suffered themselves, through the power of the devil, to be overcome, and to deny the truth and defy my power—

They are they who are the sons of perdition, of whom I say that it had been better for them never to have been born.

For they are vessels of wrath, doomed to suffer the wrath of God, with the devil and his angels in eternity;

Concerning whom I have said there is no forgiveness in this world nor in the world to come,

Having denied the Holy Spirit after having received it, and having denied the Only Begotten Son of the Father—having crucified him unto themselves, and put him to an open shame.

These are they who shall go away into the lake of fire and brimstone, with the devil and his angels,

And the only ones on whom the second death shall have any power;

Yea, verily, the only ones who shall not be redeemed in the due time of the Lord, after the sufferings of his wrath;

For all the rest shall be brought forth by the resurrection of the dead, through the triumph and the glory of the Lamb, who was slain, who was in the bosom of the Father before the worlds were made.

And this is the gospel, the glad tidings which the voice out of the heavens bore record unto us,

That he came into the world, even Jesus, to be crucified for the world, and to bear the sins of the world, and to sanctify the world, and to cleanse it from all unrighteousness;

That through him all might be saved whom the Father had put into his power and made by him,

Who glorifies the Father, and saves all the works of his hands, except those sons of perdition, who deny the Son after the Father has revealed him;

Wherefore, he saves all except them; they shall go away into everlasting punishment, which is endless punishment, which is eternal punishment, to reign with the devil, and his angels in eternity, where their worm dieth not, and the fire is not quenched, which is their torment;

And the end thereof, neither the place thereof, nor their torment, no man knows,

THE DEGREES OF GLORY

Neither was it revealed, neither is, neither will be revealed unto man, except to them who are made partakers thereof;

Nevertheless I, the Lord, show it by vision unto many, but straightway shut it up again;

Wherefore the end, the width, the height, the depth, and the misery thereof, they understand not, neither any man except them who are ordained unto this condemnation.

And we heard the voice, saying, Write the vision, for lo! this is the end of the vision of the sufferings of the ungodly!

And again, we bear record, for we saw and heard, and this is the testimony of the gospel of Christ, concerning them who come forth in the resurrection of the just;

They are they who received the testimony of Jesus, and believed on his name and were baptized after the manner of his burial, being buried in the water in his name, and this according to the commandment which he has given,

That by keeping the commandments they might be washed and cleansed from all their sins, and receive the Holy Spirit by the laying on of the hands of him who is ordained and sealed unto this power,

And who overcome by faith, and are sealed by the Holy Spirit of promise, which the Father sheds forth upon all those who are just and true.

They are they who are the church of the first born.

They are they into whose hands the Father has given all things—

They are they who are Priests and Kings, who have received of his fullness, and of his glory,

And are Priests of the Most High, after the order of Melchisedek, which was after the order of Enoch, which was after the order of the Only Begotten Son;

Wherefore, as it is written, they are Gods, even the sons of God—

Wherefore all things are theirs, whether life or death, or things present, or things to come, all are theirs, and they are Christ's and Christ is God's;

And they shall overcome all things;

THE VISION

Wherefore let no man glory in man, but rather let him glory in God who shall subdue all enemies under his feet—

These shall dwell in the presence of God and his Christ for ever and ever.

These are they whom he shall bring with him, when he shall come in the clouds of heaven, to reign on the earth over his people.

These are they who shall have part in the first resurrection.

These are they who shall come forth in the resurrection of the just.

These are they who are come unto Mount Zion, and unto the city of the living God, the heavenly place, the holiest of all,

These are they who have come to an innumerable company of angels, to the general assembly and church of Enoch, and of the first born.

These are they whose names are written in heaven, where God and Christ are the judge of all.

These are they who are just men made perfect through Jesus the mediator of the new covenant, who wrought out this perfect atonement through the shedding of his own blood.

These are they whose bodies are celestial, whose glory is that of the sun, even the glory of God, the highest of all, whose glory the sun of the firmament is written of as being typical.

And again, we saw the terrestrial world, and behold and lo, these are they who are of the terrestrial, whose glory differs from that of the church of the first born, who have received the fulness of the Father, even as that of the moon differs from the sun in the firmament.

Behold, these are they who died without law,

And also they who are the spirits of men kept in prison, whom the Son visited, and preached the gospel unto them, that they might be judged according to men in the flesh,

Who received not the testimony of Jesus in the flesh, but afterwards received it.

These are they who are honorable men of the earth, who were blinded by the craftiness of men.

These are they who receive of his glory, but not of his fullness.

THE DEGREES OF GLORY

These are they who receive of the presence of the Son, but not of the fullness of the Father;

Wherefore they are bodies terrestrial, and not bodies celestial, and differ in glory as the moon differs from the sun.

These are they who are not valiant in the testimony of Jesus; wherefore they obtain not the crown over the kingdom of our God.

And now this is the end of the vision which we saw of the terrestrial, that the Lord commanded us to write while we were yet in the Spirit.

And again, we saw the glory of the telestial, which glory is that of the lesser, even as the glory of the stars differs from that of the glory of the moon in the firmament.

These are they who received not the gospel of Christ, neither the testimony of Jesus.

These are they who deny not the Holy Spirit.

These are they who are thrust down to hell.

These are they who shall not be redeemed from the devil, until the last resurrection, until the Lord, even Christ the Lamb shall have finished his work.

These are they who receive not of his fullness in the eternal world, but of the Holy Spirit through the ministration of the terrestrial;

And the terrestrial through the ministration of the celestial;

And also the telestial receive it of the administering of angels who are appointed to minister for them, or who are appointed to be ministering spirits for them, for they shall be heirs of salvation.

And thus we saw in the heavenly vision, the glory of the telestial, which surpasses all understanding.

And no man knows it except him to whom God has revealed it.

And thus we saw the glory of the terrestrial, which excels in all things the glory of the telestial, even in glory, and in power, and in might, and in dominion.

And thus we saw the glory of the celestial, which excels in all things—where God, even the father, reigns upon his throne for ever and ever;

[7]

THE VISION

Before whose throne all things bow in humble reverence and give him glory for ever and ever.

They who dwell in his presence are the church of the first born, and they see as they are seen, and know as they are known, having received of his fullness and of his grace;

And he makes them equal in power, and in might, and in dominion.

And the glory of the celestial is one, even as the glory of the sun is one.

And the glory of the terrestrial is one, even as the glory of the moon is one.

And the glory of the telestial is one, even as the glory of the stars is one, for as one star differs from another star in glory, even so differs one from another in glory in the telestial world;

For these are they who are of Paul, and of Apollos, and of Cephas.

These are they who say they are some of one and some of another—some of Christ, and some of John, and some of Moses and some of Elias, and some of Esaias, and some of Isaiah, and some of Enoch;

But received not the gospel, neither the testimony of Jesus, neither the prophets, neither the everlasting covenant.

Last of all, these all are they who will not be gathered with the saints, to be caught up unto the church of the first born, and received into the cloud.

These are they who are liars, and sorcerers, and adulterers, and whoremongers, and whosoever loves and makes a lie.

These are they who suffer the wrath of God on the earth.

These are they who suffer the vengeance of eternal fire.

These are they who are cast down to hell and suffer the wrath of Almighty God, until the fullness of times when Christ shall have subdued all enemies under his feet, and shall have perfected his work.

When he shall deliver up the kingdom, and present it unto the Father spotless, saying—I have overcome and have trodden the wine-press alone, even the wine-press of the fierceness of the wrath of Almighty God.

THE DEGREES OF GLORY

Then shall he be crowned with the crown of his glory, to sit on the throne of his power to reign for ever and ever.

But behold, and lo, we saw the glory and the inhabitants of the telestial world, that they were as innumerable as the stars in the firmament of heaven, or as the sand upon the sea shore,

And heard the voice of the Lord, saying—these all shall bow the knee, and every tongue shall confess to him who sits upon the throne for ever and ever;

For they shall be judged according to their works, and every man shall receive according to his own works, his own dominion, in the mansions which are prepared,

And they shall be servants of the Most High, but where God and Christ dwell they cannot come, worlds without end.

This is the end of the vision which we saw, which we were commanded to write while we were yet in the Spirit.

But great and marvelous are the works of the Lord, and the mysteries of his kingdom which he showed unto us, which surpasses all understanding in glory, and in might, and in dominion,

Which he commanded us we should not write while we were yet in the Spirit, and not lawful for man to utter;

Neither is man capable to make them known, for they are only to be seen, and understood by the power of the Holy Spirit, which God bestows on those who love him, and purify themselves before him;

To whom he grants this privilege of seeing and knowing for themselves;

That through the power and manifestation of the Spirit, while in the flesh, they may be able to bear his presence in the world of glory.

And to God and the Lamb be glory, and honor, and dominion for ever and ever. Amen."

Documentary History of Church, Vol. 1, pp. 245-252.

"THE VISION"—A TRANSCRIPT FROM THE RECORDS OF THE ETERNAL WORLD

"Nothing could be more pleasing to the Saints upon the order of the Kingdom of the Lord, than the light which burst upon the world through the foregoing vision. Every law, every commandment, every promise, every truth, and every point touching the destiny of man, from Genesis to Revelation, where the purity of the Scriptures remains unsullied by the folly of men, go to show the perfection of the theory (of different degrees of glory in the future life) and witnesses the fact that that document is a transcript from the records of the eternal world. The sublimity of the ideas; the purity of the language; the scope for action; the continued duration for completion, in order that the heirs of salvation may confess the Lord and bow the knee; the rewards for faithfulness, and the punishments for sins, are so much beyond the narrow-mindedness of men, that every honest man is constrained to exclaim: 'It came from God'."—*Joseph Smith.*

Documentary History of Church, Vol. 1, *p.* 252.

꒰ꔛ

JOSEPH THE PROPHET NOT PERMITTED TO REVEAL ONE-HUNDREDTH PART OF WHAT HE SAW IN "THE VISION"

"In a discourse which Joseph delivered on the 21st day of May, 1843, to a large congregation in Nauvoo, he said:

"I love that man better who swears a stream as long as my arm, yet deals justice to his neighbors and mercifully deals his substance to the poor, than the long, smooth-faced hypocrite * *

"God judges men according to the use they make of the light which He gives them. * * *

"*I could explain a hundredfold more than I ever have of the glories of the kingdoms manifested to me in the vision, were I permitted, and were the people prepared to receive it.* * * *

"Salvation is for a man to be saved from all his enemies; for until a man can triumph over death, he is not saved. A knowledge of the Priesthood alone will do this."

Historical Record, p. 515.

THE DEGREES OF GLORY

THE PLACE WHERE "THE VISION" WAS GIVEN

Testimony of Philo Dibble*

"When Joseph was ready to go back to Hiram, I took him in my carriage. Soon afterwards I had occasion to visit Hiram again. On my way there I was persuaded to stop at the Hulet Settlement and attend a meeting. When I arrived at Father Johnson's the next morning Joseph and Sidney had just finished washing up from being tarred and feathered the night before. Joseph said to Sidney: "We can now go on our mission to Jackson county" (alluding to a commandment given them while they were translating but which they concluded not to attend to until they had finished that work). I felt to regret very much that I had not been with them the evening before but it was perhaps providential that I was not. On a subsequent visit to Hiram I arrived at Father Johnson's just as Joseph and Sidney were coming out of the vision alluded to in the book of Doctrine and Covenants, in which mention is made of the three glories. Joseph wore black clothes but at this time seemed to be dressed in an element of glorious white, and his face shown as if it were transparent, but I did not see the same glory attending Sidney. Joseph appeared as strong as a lion but Sidney seemed as weak as water, and Joseph noticing his condition smiled and said: "Brother Sidney is not as used to it as I am."

Eighth Book of Faith-Promoting Series, pp. 80-81.

---

*IMPORTANT STATEMENT BY THE PROPHET JOSEPH: Mrs. Sarah N. Williams Reynolds, of Salt Lake City, dictated the following highly important statement to the Compiler of this book: "I was a close neighbor of Philo Dibble who visited me very often. He had been very familiar and intimately acquainted with the Prophet Joseph Smith, and took great delight in rehearsing his wealth of information concerning this acquaintance. Brother Dibble stated to me that the Prophet Joseph told him in connection with the others who were present in Father Johnson's home at the time the Vision was given to the Prophet Joseph and Sidney Rigdon, that (the Prophet speaking): 'MY WHOLE BODY WAS FULL OF LIGHT AND I COULD SEE EVEN OUT AT THE ENDS OF MY FINGERS AND TOES'."

For additional light upon this highly important subject, consult Orson Pratt's masterful discourse on "The Increased Powers and Faculties of the Mind in a Future State" found in the compilation entitled: Temples of the most High — pages 276-7.

THE IMPORTANCE PLACED ON "THE VISION"

By President Wilford Woodruff

(Excerpts from sermon delivered at the Bear Lake Stake Conference, Paris, Idaho, on Monday afternoon, August 10, 1891.)

"I had read "THE VISION" recorded in this Book of Doctrine and Covenants, and it had given me more light and more knowledge with regard to the dealings of God with men than all the revelations I had ever read, in the Bible or anywhere else. I had been taught that there was one heaven and one hell; and everybody that was not sprinkled or baptized, infants and all, would have to go to hell. It made no difference whether the individual had committed no wrong, if he had not been received into the church by sprinkling or baptism, he would have to go to hell with the murderer, with the whoremonger, with the wickedest of men. On the other hand, everybody that was sprinkled would go to heaven. No matter if they had never made a single sacrifice for the Gospel of Christ, they would have the same glory as Peter, James and John, who had sacrificed their lives for the Gospel's sake. That was the kind of teaching I heard in my boyhood. I did not believe one word of it then; and I don't now. But this vision of which I speak opened my eyes. It showed me the power of God and the righteousness of God in dealing with the human family. Before I saw Joseph I said I did not care how old he was, or how young he was; I did not care how he looked—whether his hair was long or short; the man that advanced that revelation was a prophet of God. I knew it for myself."

Deseret Weekly News, Vol. 43, No. 2, p. 321.

TESTIMONY OF ORSON PRATT CONCERNING "THE VISION"

(Excerpt from sermon delivered in the Thirteenth Ward Assembly Rooms, Sunday evening, August 25, 1878.)

Then again, what could we learn from either the Bible or Book of Mormon in regard to three glories—the celestial, the terrestrial and the telestial glories. What did we know concerning those that should inherit these various worlds of glory? Nothing at all. It was merely referred to in Paul's writings, that there were three glories, "one glory of the sun, and another glory of the moon, and another glory of the stars, for one star differeth from another star in glory, so also is the resurrection of the dead." But Paul left us there; he did not tell us anything about the celestial, or anything about terrestrial, or telestial glories; he told us nothing about the inhabitants of these worlds, nor anything about the laws by which these different glorified worlds were governed, but merely referred to them in a few words and then dropped it. The people, to whom he was writing may have known all about the subject he so casually referred to; if they did, the knowledge they possessed was not handed down to us. But the Lord, on the 16th day of February, 1832, poured out his spirit from on high while Joseph was engaged in the work of translating another record, and also upon his scribe, and they saw in vision the celestial world, and they were commanded to write a portion of the things which they saw; to write about the greatness and power and majesty and the knowledge of the people who inherit the celestial world. And they were also shown, in the same manner the terrestrial world and the inhabitants thereof and their glory, and what their condition would be in the eternal worlds; and then they descended also in their vision and beheld the lesser or telestial glory, and they saw the inhabitants that dwelt there and comprehended the laws by which they were governed. Some of these things they were commanded to write while there were things which they beheld which they were strictly commanded not to write, as the world was not worthy to receive them. Neither was the Church, at that time, prepared to receive a full knowledge concerning these things. But that portion which they were permitted to write they wrote, and it has been printed now some forty years for the Saints and for the inhabitants of the world to learn concerning the future condition of all those that shall pass out of this state of existence behind the veil."

J.-D., Vol. 20, p. 70.

THE VISION

TESTIMONY OF SIDNEY RIGDON

(From sermon delivered at Nauvoo, April 6, 1844.)

"If any man says it is not the work of God, I know he lies. Some of you who know you have a house, how long would it take to make you reason yourselves into belief that you have no house where you now reside with your families? Neither have we any power whereby we can ever persuade ourselves that this is not the Church of God. We do not care who sinks or swims, or opposes, but we know here is the Church of God, and I have authority before God for saying so. I have the testimony of Jesus, which is the spirit of prophecy. I have slept with it—I have walked with it. The idea has never been out of my heart for a moment, and I will reap the glory of it when I leave this world. I defy man and hell and devils to put it out of my heart. I defy all, and will triumph in spite of all of them. I know God. I have gazed upon the glory of God, the throne; the visions, and glories of God, and the visions of eternity in the days gone by."

&

THE KING FOLLETT DISCOURSE
(Excerpts)
(With footnotes by Pres. B. H. Roberts)

President Joseph Smith delivered the following discourse before about twenty thousand Saints at the April Conference of the Church, 1844, being the funeral sermon of Elder King Follett.

Reported by Willard Richards, Wilford Woodruff, Thomas Bullock, and William Clayton.* This discourse was first published in the "Times and Seasons" of August 1, 1844.

---

*It must be remembered that the report of the Prophet's speech, made by the brethren above named, was not a stenographic report, but one made in longhand, and afterwards perfected as nearly as possible by consultation and mutual correcting and development of each other's notes. It may, therefore, be concluded that there are some imperfections in the report of this discourse which one here and there feels, since at some points the matter is not absolutely clear or the thought not completely rounded out. For a further discussion and illustration of the matter, see the History of the Church, vol. iv, pp. 556-7.

THE DEGREES OF GLORY

Beloved Saints: I will call (require) the attention of this congregation while I address you on the subject of the dead. The decease of our beloved brother, Elder King Follett, who was crushed in a well by the falling of a tub of rock, has more immediately led me to that subject. I have been requested to speak by his friends and relatives, but inasmuch as there are a great many in this congregation who live in this city as well as elsewhere, who have lost friends, I feel disposed to speak on the subject in general, and offer you my ideas, so far as I have ability, and so far as I shall be inspired by the Holy Spirit to dwell on this subject. . . .

Before I enter fully into the investigation of the subject which is lying before me, I wish to pave the way and bring up the subject from the beginning, that you may understand it. I will make a few preliminaries, in order that you may understand the subject when I come to it. I do not calculate or intend to please your ears with superfluity of words or oratory, or with much learning; but I calculate (intend) to edify you with the simple truths from heaven.

In the first place, I wish to go back to the beginning—to the morn of creation. There is the starting point for us to look to, in order to understand and be fully acquainted with the mind, purposes and decrees of the Great Eloheim, who sits in yonder heavens as he did at the creation of this world. It is necessary for us to have an understanding of God himself in the beginning. If we start right, it is easy to go right all the time; but if we start wrong, we may go wrong, and it will be a hard matter to get right.

There are but a very few beings in the world who understand rightly the character of God. The great majority of mankind do not comprehend anything, either that which is past, or that which is to come, as it respects their relationship to God. They do not know, neither do they understand the nature of that relationship and consequently they know but little above the brute beast, or more than to eat, drink and sleep. This is all man knows about God or his existence, unless it is given by the inspiration of the Almighty.

If a man learns nothing more than to eat, drink and sleep,

[15]

and does not comprehend any of the designs of God, the beast comprehends the same things. It eats, drinks, sleeps, and knows nothing more about God; yet it knows as much as we, unless we are able to comprehend by the inspiration of Almighty God. If men do not comprehend the character of God, they do not comprehend themselves.* I want to go back to the beginning, and so lift your minds into a more lofty sphere and a more exalted understanding than what the human mind generally aspires to.

I want to ask this congregation, every man, woman and child, to answer the question in his own heart, what kind of a being God is? Ask yourselves; turn your thoughts into your hearts, and say if any of you have seen, heard or communed with him. This is a question that may occupy your attention for a long time. I again repeat the question—What kind of a being is God? Does any man or woman know? Have any of you seen him, heard him, or communed with him? Here is the question that will, peradventure, from this time henceforth occupy your attention. The scriptures inform us that "This is life eternal that they might know thee, the only true God, and Jesus Christ whom thou hast sent."

If any man does not know God, and inquires what kind of a being he is—if he will search diligently his own heart—if the declaration of Jesus and the apostles be true, he will realize that he has not eternal life; for there can be eternal life on no other principle.   *   *   *   *

*This is somewhat at variance with Pope's admonition—
   Know then thyself, presume not God to scan:
   The proper study for mankind is man.

Reflection on the Prophet's utterance, however, will justify his doctrine. Man will remain a mystery to himself until he has mastered somewhat the mystery of God. An understanding of each is essential to the understanding of the other. "And this is life eternal, that they might know thee, the only true God, and Jesus Christ whom thou hast sent" (St. John 17). It is clearly, then, within the spiritual economy of God that men shall know him, for upon that fact depends eternal life. Moreover, though it may be admitted without controversy that "great is the mystery of Godliness" yet "God was manifested (marginal reading) in the flesh, justified in the Spirit, seen of angels, preached unto the Gentiles, believed on in the world, received up into glory—" (I Tim. 3:16)—all in plain allusion to the Christ, who was, therefore, God manifested (i. e. revealed) in the flesh; so that all may know God through Jesus Christ; and by understanding him, understand God and thus lay the foundation of better self-knowledge.

THE DEGREES OF GLORY

I will go back to the beginning before the world was, to show what kind of a being God is. What sort a being was God in the beginning? Open your ears and hear, all ye ends of the earth, for I am going to prove it to you by the Bible, and tell you the designs of God in relation to the human race and why he interferes with the affairs of man.

God himself was once as we are now, and is an exalted man and sits enthroned in yonder heavens! That is the great secret. If the vail were rent today, and the great God who holds this world in its orbit, and who upholds all worlds and all things by his power, was to make himself visible—I say, if you were to see him today, you would see him like a man in form—like yourselves in all the person, image, and very form as a man; for Adam was created in the very fashion, image and likeness of God, and received instruction from, and walked, talked, and conversed with him, as one man talks and communes with another.

In order to understand the subject of the dead for the consolation of those who mourn for the loss of their friends, it is necessary that we should understand the character and being of God and how he came to be so; for I am going to tell you how God came to be God. We have imagined and supposed that God was God from all eternity. I will refute that idea and take away the veil, so that you may see.

These are incomprehensible ideas to some, but they are simple. *It is the first principle of the gospel to know for a certainty the character of God, and to know that we may converse with him as one man converses with another, and that he was once a man like us;* yea, that God himself, the father of us all, dwelt on an earth, the same as Jesus Christ himself did; and I will show it from the Bible.*

I wish I was in a suitable place to tell it, and that I had the

---

*The doctrine here taught was afterwards thrown into the following aphorism by Lorenzo Snow:

As man now is, God once was;
As God now is, man may become.

This form of expressing the truth was doubtless original with Lorenzo Snow, but not the doctrine itself. That is contained in the Prophet's remarks above, text and context.

THE VISION

trumpet of an archangel, so that I could tell the story in such a manner that persecution would cease forever. What did Jesus say? (Mark it, Elder Rigdon!) The scriptures inform us that Jesus said, As the Father hath power in himself, even so hath the Son power—to do what? Why, what the Father did. The answer is obvious—in a manner to lay down his body and take it up again. Jesus, what are you going to do? To lay down my life as my Father did, and take it up again. Do you believe it? If you do not believe it you do not believe the Bible.* The scriptures say it and I defy all the learning and wisdom and all the combined powers of earth and hell together to refute it.

Here, then, is eternal life—to know the only wise and true God; and you have got to learn how to be Gods yourselves, and to be kings and priests to God, the same as all Gods have done before you,† namely, by going from one small degree to another,

---

*The argument here made by the Prophet is very much strengthened by the following passage: "The Son can do nothing of himself, but what he seeth the Father do; for what things soever he (the Father) doeth, these also doeth the Son likewise." (St. John 5·19.)

†Perhaps no passage in the Prophet's discourse has given more offense than the one here noted, and yet men are coming to think and feel the truth of what he said.   Henry Drummond, for instance (following the Prophet by half a century), in his really great work, "Natural Law in the Spiritual World," in the chapter on Growth, wherein he points out the difference between the merely mortal man and one whose life has been touched by the spiritual power of God, and so received something that the merely mortal man has not received, says: "The end of salvation is perfection, the Christ-like mind, character and life. * * * Therefore the man who has within himself this great formative agent, Life (spiritual life), is nearer the end than the man who has mortality alone. The latter can never reach perfection, the former must. For the life must develop out according to its type; and being a germ of the Christ-life, it must unfold into a Christ."   Joseph Smith's doctrine means no more than this.

Sir Oliver Lodge says much to the same effect in the following passage on "Christianity and Science." (Hibbert's Journal, April, 1906):

"It is orthodox, therefore, to maintain that Christ's birth was miraculous and his death portentous, that he continued in existence otherwise than as we men continue, that his very body rose and ascended into heaven—whatever that collocation of words may mean.   But I suggest that such an attempt at exceptional glorification of his body is a pious heresy—a heresy which misses the truth lying open to our eyes. His humanity is to be recognized as real and ordinary and thorough and complete; not in the middle life alone; but at birth, and at death and after death.   Whatever happened to him may happen to any one of us, provided we attain the appropriate altitude; an altitude which, whether within our individual reach or not, is assuredly within reach of humanity.   That is what he urged again and again.   "Be born again." "Be ye perfect."   "Ye are the sons of God."   "My Father and your Father, my God and your God."   The un-uniqueness of the ordinary humanity of Christ is the first

[18]

and from a small capacity to a great one; from grace to grace, from exaltation to exaltation, until you attain to the resurrection of the dead, and are able to dwell in everlasting burnings, and to sit in glory, as do those who sit enthroned in everlasting power. And I want you to know that God, in the last days, while certain individuals are proclaiming his name, is not trifling with you or me.

These are the first principles of consolation. How consoling to the mourners when they are called to part with a husband, wife, father, mother, child, or dear relative, to know that, although the earthly tabernacle is laid down and dissolved, they shall rise again to dwell in everlasting burnings in immortal glory, not to sorrow, suffer, or die any more; but they shall be heirs of God and joint heirs with Jesus Christ. What is it? To inherit the same power, the same glory and the same exaltation, until you arrive at the station of a God, and ascend the throne of eternal power, the same as those who have gone before. What did Jesus do? Why; I do the things I saw my Father do when worlds came rolling into existence. My Father worked out His kingdom with fear and trembling, and I must do the same; and when I get my Kingdom, I shall present it to my Father, so that he may obtain kingdom upon kingdom, and it will exalt him in glory. He will then take a higher exaltation, and I will take his place, and thereby become exalted myself. So that Jesus treads in the tracks of his Father, and inherits what God himself did before; and God is thus glorified and exalted in the salvation and exaltation of all his children. It is plain beyond disputation, and you thus learn some of the first principles of the gospel, about which so much hath been said.

---

patent truth, masked only by well-meaning and reverent superstition. But the second truth is greater than that—without it the first would be meaningless and useless,— if man alone, what gain have we? The world is full of men. What the world wants is a God. Behold the God!—(that is, the God, Jesus Christ.)

The divinity of Jesus is the truth which now requires to be reperceived, to be illumined afresh by new knowledge, to be cleansed and revivified by the wholesome flood of scepticism which has poured over it; it can be freed now from all trace of grovelling superstition; and can be recognized freely and enthusiastically; the divinity of Jesus, and (the divinity) of all other noble and saintly souls, in so far as they, too, have been inflamed by a spark of Deity—in so far as they, too, can be recognized as manifestations of the Divine.

THE VISION

When you climb up a ladder, you must begin at the bottom, and ascend step by step, until you arrive at the top; and so it is with the principles of the gospel—you must begin with the first, and go on until you learn all the principles of exaltation. But it will be a great while after you have passed through the veil before you will have learned them. It is not all to be comprehended in this world; it will be a great work to learn our salvation and exaltation even beyond the grave. I suppose that I am not allowed to go into an investigation of anything that is not contained in the Bible. If I do, I think there are so many over-wise men here, that they would cry "treason" and put me to death. So I will go to the old Bible and turn commentator today.

I shall comment on the very first Hebrew word in the Bible; I will make a comment on the very first sentence of the history of creation in the Bible—*Berosheit.* I want to analyze the word. *Baith*—in, by, through, and everything else. *Rosh*—the head. *Sheit*—grammatical termination. When the inspired man wrote it, he did not put the *baith* there. An old Jew without any authority added the word; he thought it too bad to begin to talk about the head! It read first, "The head one of the Gods brought forth the Gods." That is the true meaning of the words. *Baurau* signifies to bring forth. If you do not believe it, you do not believe the learned men of God. Learned men can teach you no more than what I have told you. *Thus the head God brought forth the Gods in the grand council.* * * * *

In the beginning, the head of the Gods called a council of the Gods; and they came together and concocted a plan to create the world and people it. When we begin to learn this way, we begin to learn the only true God, and what kind of being we have got to worship. Having a knowledge of God, we begin to know how to approach him, and how to ask so as to receive an answer.

When we understand the character of God, and know how to come to him, he begins to unfold the heavens to us, and to tell us all about it. When we are ready to come to him, he is ready to come to us.

Now, I ask all who hear me why the learned men who are preaching salvation, say that God created the heavens and the earth out of nothing? The reason is, that they are unlearned in the things of God, and have not the gift of the Holy Ghost; they account it blasphemy in any one to contradict their idea. If you tell them that God made the world out of something, they will call you a fool. But I am learned and know more than all the world put together. The Holy Ghost does, anyhow, and he is within me and comprehends more than all the world; and I will associate myself with him.

You ask the learned doctors why they say the world was made out of nothing, and they will answer, "Doesn't the Bible say he *created* the world?" And they infer, from the word create, that it must have been made out of nothing. Now, the word create came from the word *baurau,* which does not mean to create out of nothing; it means to organize; the same as a man would organize materials and build a ship.*

---

*The views of the Prophet on this subject of creation is abundantly sustained by by men of learning subsequent to his time. The Rev. Baden Powell of Oxford University, for instance, writing for Kitto's Cyclopaedia of Biblical Literature, says: "The meaning of this word (create) has been commonly associated with the idea of 'making out of nothing.' But when we come to inquire more precisely into the subject, we can, of course, satisfy ourselves as to the meaning only from an examination of the original phrase." The learned professor then proceeds to say that three distinct Hebrew verbs are in different places employed with reference to the same divine act, and may be translated, respectively, create, make, "form or fashion." "Now," continues the professor, "though each of these has its shade of distinction, yet the best critics understand them as so nearly synonymous that, at least in regard to the idea of making out of nothing, little or no foundation for that doctrine can be obtained from the first of these words—viz., the verb translated "create," then the chances are still less for there being any foundation for the doctrine of creation from nothing in the verb translated, "made," "formed" or "fashioned."

Professor Powell further says: "The idea of 'creation,' as meaning absolutely 'making out of nothing,' or calling into existence that which did not exist before, in the strictest sense of the term, is not a doctrine of scripture but it has been held by many on the grounds of natural theology, as enhancing the ideas we form of the divine power, and more specially since the contrary must imply the belief in the eternality and self-existence of matter."

Dr. William Smith's great dictionary of the Bible (Hackett edition, 1894) has no article on the term "create" or "creation," but in the article "earth" we have reference to the subject, and really an implied explanation as to why this work contains no treatise on "create" or "creation." "The act of creation itself, as recorded in the first chapter of Genesis, is a subject beyond and above the experience of man; human language, derived, as it originally was, from the sensible and material world, fails to find an adequate term to describe the act; for our word 'create' and the Hebrew *bara,* though most appropriate to express the idea of an original creation; are yet applicable and must necessarily be applicable to other modes of creation; nor does the addition of such expressions as 'out of things that were not,' or 'not from things which appear,' contribute much to the force of the declaration. The absence of a term which shall describe exclusively an original creation is a neces-

[21]

THE VISION

Hence we infer that God had materials to organize the world out of chaos—chaotic matter, which is element and in which dwells all the glory. Element had an existence from the time he had. The pure principles of element are principles which can never be destroyed; and they may be organized and reorganized, but not destroyed. They had no beginning, and can have no end.*

I have another subject to dwell upon, which is calculated to exalt man; but it is impossible for me to say much on this subject; I shall therefore just touch upon it, for time will not

sary infirmity of language; as the events occurred but once, the corresponding term must, in order to be adequate, have been coined for the occasion and reserved for it alone, which would have been impossible."

The philosophers with equal emphasis sustain the contention of the Prophet. Herbert Spencer, in his "First Principles," (1860), said:

"There was once universally current, a notion that things could vanish into absolute nothing, or arise out of absolute nothing. * * * The current theology, in its teachings respecting the beginning and the end of the world, is clearly pervaded by it. * * * The gradual accumulation of experiences has tended slowly to reverse this conviction; until now, the doctrine that matter is indestructible has become a commonplace. All the apparent proofs that something can come out of nothing, a wider knowledge has one by one cancelled. The comet that is suddenly discovered in the heavens and nightly waxes larger, is proved not to be a newly-created body, but a body that was until lately beyond the range of vision. The cloud which in the course of a few minutes forms in the sky, consists not of substance that has just begun to be, but of substance that previously existed in a more diffused and transparent form. And similarly with a crystal or precipitate in relation to the fluid depositing it. Conversely, the seeming annihilations of matter turn out, on closer observation, to be only changes of state. It is found that the evaporated water, though it has become invisible, may be brought by condensation to its original shape. The discharged fowling-piece gives evidence that though the gunpowder has disappeared, there have appeared in place of it certain gases, which, in assuming a larger volume, have caused the explosion."

Fiske follows Spencer, of course, and in his "Cosmic Philosophy" sums up the matter in these words: "It is now inconceivable that a particle of matter should either come into existence, or lapse into non-existence."

Robert Kennedy Duncan (1905), in his "New Knowledge," says: "Governing matter in all its varied forms, there is one great fundamental law which up to this time has been ironclad in its character. This law, known as the law of the conservation of mass, states that no particle of matter, however small, may be created or destroyed. All the king's horses and all the king's men cannot destroy a pin's head. We may smash that pin's head, dissolve it in acid, burn it in the electric furnace, employ, in a word, every annihilating agency, and yet that pin's head persists in being. Again, it is as uncreatable as it is indestructible. In other words, we cannot create something out of nothing. The material must be furnished for every existent article. The sum of matter in the universe is x-pounds—and, while it may be carried through a myriad of forms, when all is said and done, it is just—x-pounds."

*"The elements are eternal, and spirit and element inseparably connected receive a fullness of joy. * * * The elements are the tabernacle of God; yea, man is the tabernacle of God, even temples."—Doc. and Cov., sec. 93:35.

permit me to say all. It is associated with the subject of the resurrection of the dead,—namely, the soul—the mind of man— the immortal spirit. Where did it come from? All learned men and doctors of divinity say that God created it in the beginning; but it is not so:† the very idea lessens man in my estimation. I do not believe the doctrine: I know better. Hear it, all ye ends of the world; for God has told me so; and if you don't believe me, it will not make the truth without effect. I will make a man appear a fool before I get through if he does not believe it. I am going to tell of things more noble.

We say that God himself is a self-existent being. Who told you so? It is correct enough; but how did it get into your heads? Who told you that man did not exist in like manner upon the same principles? Man does exist upon the same principles. God made a tabernacle and put a spirit into it, and it became a living soul. (Refers to the old Bible.) How does it read in the Hebrew? It does not say in the Hebrew that God created the spirit of man. It says, "God made man out of earth and put into him Adam's spirit, and so became a living body."

The mind or the intelligence which man possesses is co-equal* with God himself. I know that my testimony is true; hence, when I talk to these mourners, what have they lost? Their relatives and friends are only separated from their bodies

---

†"I (the Christ) was in the beginning with the Father, and was the first born. * * * Ye (addressing the brethren present when the revelation was being received)—ye were also in the beginning with the Father; that which is spirit (i. e., that part of the brethren that was spirit), even the spirit of truth. * * * Man (the race, all men, the term man is generic)—man was also in the beginning with God. Intelligence (meaning doubtless the intelligent entity in each man—all intelligences) intelligence, or the light of truth, was not created or made, neither indeed can be."—Doc. and Cov., sec. 113. Hence the self-existence, and necessarily the eternal existence, and uncreatableness of the minds or intelligences of men, for which the Prophet is contending in his discourse.

*Undoubtedly the proper word here would be "co-eternal," not "co-equal." This illustrates the imperfection of the report made of the sermon. For surely the mind of man is not co-equal with God except in the matter of its eternity. It is the direct statement in the Book of Abraham—accepted by the Church as scripture—that there are differences in the intelligences that exist, that some are more intelligent than others; and that God is "more intelligent than they all"— Book of Abraham, chapt. 3. I believe that this means more than that God is more intelligent than any other one of the intelligences. It means that he is more intelligent than all of the other intelligences combined. His intelligence is

THE VISION

for a short season: their spirits which existed with God have left the tabernacle of clay only for a little moment, as it were; and they now exist in a place where they converse together the same as we do on the earth.

I am dwelling on the immortality of the spirit of man. Is it logical to say that the intelligence of spirits is immortal, and yet that it had a beginning? The intelligence of spirits had no beginning, neither will it have an end. That is good logic. That which has a beginning may have an end. There never was a time when there were not spirits; for they are co-equal (co-eternal) with our Father in Heaven.

I want to reason more on the spirit of man; for I am dwelling on the body and spirit of man—on the subject of the dead. I take my ring from my finger and liken it unto the mind of man—the immortal part, because it has no beginning. Suppose you cut it in two; then it has a beginning and an end; but join it again, and it continues one eternal round. So with the spirit of man. As the Lord liveth, if it had a beginning, it will have an end. All the fools and learned and wise men from the beginning of creation, who say that the spirit of man had a beginning, prove that it must have an end; and if that doctrine is true, then the doctrine of annihilation would be true. But if I am right, I might with boldness proclaim from the house-tops that God never had the power to create the spirit of man at all. God himself could not create himself.

Intelligence is eternal and exists upon a self-existent prin-

---

greater than that of the mass, and that has led me to say in the second Year Book of the Seventies: "It is this fact doubtless which makes this One, 'more intelligent than they all'." God. He is the All-Wise-One! The All-Powerful-One! What he tells other Intelligences to do must be precisely the wisest, fittest thing that they could anywhere or anyhow learn—the thing which will always behoove them, with right loyal thankfulness, and nothing doubting, to do. There goes with this, too, the thought that this All-Wise-One will be the Unselfish One, the All-Loving-One, the One who desires that which is highest, and best; not for himself alone, but for all; and that will be best for him, too. His glory, his power, his joy will be enhanced by the uplifting of all, by enlarging them; by increasing their joy, power, and glory. And because this All-Intelligent One is all this, and does all this, the other Intelligences worship him, submit their judgments and their will to his judgment and his will. He knows, and can do that which is best; and this submission of the mind to the Most Intelligent, Wisest—wiser than all—is worship. This the whole meaning of the doctrine and the life of Christ expressed in—"Father, not my will, but Thy will be done."

ciple. It is a spirit* from age to age, and there is no creation about it. All the minds and spirits that God ever sent into the world are susceptible of enlargement.†

The first principles of man are self-existent with God. God himself, finding he was in the midst of spirits and glory, because he was more intelligent, saw proper to institute laws whereby the rest could have a privilege to advance like himself. The relationship we have with God places us in a situation to advance in knowledge. He has power to institute laws to instruct the weaker intelligences, that they may be exalted with himself, so that they might have one glory upon another, and all that knowledge, power, glory, and intelligence, which is requisite in order to save them in the world of spirits.**

* * * I want to talk more of the relation of man to God. I will open your eyes in relation to your dead. All things whatsoever God in his infinite wisdom has seen fit and proper to reveal to us, while we are dwelling in mortality, in regard to our mortal bodies, are revealed to us in the abstract, and independent of affinity of this mortal tabernacle, but are revealed to our spirits precisely as though we had no bodies at all; and those revelations, which will save our spirits will save our bodies.

---

*"A spirit from age to age"—not "spirit from age to age"; but "a spirit," that is, an entity, a person, an individual. This paragraph in the Prophet's remarks may well be taken as an interpretation of Doc. and Cov., sec. 93:29.

†"But are not creatable," would have rounded out the thought.

**"Behold this is my work and my glory, to bring to pass the immortality and eternal life of man."—(The Lord to Moses, Book of Moses, chapt. 1:39; Pearl of Great Price)—that is, "to bring to pass the immortality and eternal life of man," as man. The passage has reference doubtless to man as composed of spirit and body—a proper "soul." (See Doc. and Cov., sec. 88: 15-16)—"For the spirit and the body are the soul of man; and the resurrection of the dead is the redemption of the soul." In other words, the "work" and the "glory" of God are achieved in bringing to pass the "immortality and eternal life of man," as man, in the eternal union of the spirit and body of man through the resurrection—through the redemption of the soul. This brings into eternal union "spirit and element" declared by the word of God to be essential to a fulness of joy—"The elements are eternal, and spirit and element, inseparably connected, receive a fulness of joy; and when separated man cannot receive a fulness of joy."—Doc. and Cov., sec. 93. Also "Adam fell that men might be: and men are that they might have joy."—II Nephi 2:25. Indeed, the whole purpose of God in bringing to pass the earth life of man is to inure to the welfare and enlargement of man as urged in the teaching of the Prophet in the paragraph above. God affects man only to his advantage. See also Seventy's Year Book No. II, Lesson ii, note 6.

God reveals them to us in view of no eternal dissolution of the body, or tabernacle. Hence the responsibility, the awful responsibility, that rests upon us in relation to our dead; for all the spirits who have not obeyed the gospel in the flesh must either obey it in the spirit or be damned. Solemn thought!—dreadful thought! Is there nothing to be done?—no preparation—no salvation for our fathers and friends who have died without having had the opportunity to obey the decrees of the Son of Man? Would to God that I had forty days and nights in which to tell you all! I would let you know that I am not a "fallen prophet."*

What promises are made in relation to the subject of the salvation of the dead? and what kind of characters are those who can be saved, although their bodies are mouldering and decaying in the grave? When his commandments teach us it is in view of eternity; for we are looked upon by God as though we were in eternity. God dwells in eternity and does not view things as we do.

The greatest responsibility in this world that God has laid upon us is to seek after our dead. The Apostle says, "They without us cannot be made perfect:"** for it is necessary that the sealing power should be in our hands to seal our children and our dead for the fullness of the dispensation of time—a dispensation to meet the promises made by Jesus Christ before the foundation of the world for the salvation of man.

Now, I will speak of them. I will meet Paul half way. I say to you, Paul you cannot be perfect without us. It is necessary that those who are going before and those who come after us should have salvation in common with us; and thus God has made it obligatory upon man. Hence God said, "I will send

---

*Accusations were repeatedly being made about this time that President Smith was a fallen prophet. But when the mighty doctrines that in this discourse he is setting forth are taken into account, and the spiritual power with which he is delivering them is reckoned with, no more complete refutation of his being a fallen prophet could be made. The Prophet lived his life in *crescendo*. From small beginnings, it rose in breadth and power as he neared its close. As a teacher he reached the climax of his career in this discourse. After it there was but one thing more he could do—seal his testimony with his blood. This he did less than three months later. Such is not the manner of life of false prophets.

**Hebrews 11:40.

[26]

you Elijah the prophet before the coming of the great and dreadful day of the Lord: and he shall turn the hearts of the fathers to the children, and the hearts of the children to their fathers, lest I come and smite the earth with a curse."*

I have a declaration to make as to the provisions which God hath made to suit the conditions of man—made from before the foundation of the world. What has Jesus said? All sins, and all blasphemies, and every transgression, except one, that man can be guilty of, may be forgiven; and there is a salvation for all men, either in this world or the world to come, who have not committed the unpardonable sin, there being a provision either in this world or the world of spirits. Hence God hath made a provision that every spirit in the eternal world can be ferreted out and saved unless he has committed the unpardonable sin, which cannot be remitted to him either in this world or the world of spirits. God has wrought out a salvation for all men, unless they have committed a certain sin; and every man who has a friend in the eternal world can save him, unless he has committed the unpardonable sin. And so you can see how far you can be a savior.

A man cannot commit the unpardonable sin after the dissolution of the body, and there is a way possible for escape. Knowledge saves a man; and in the world of spirits no man can be exalted but by knowledge. So long as a man will not give heed to the commandments, he must abide without salvation. If a man has knowledge, he can be saved; although, if he has been guilty of great sins, he will be punished for them. But when he consents to obey the gospel, whether here or in the world of spirits, he is saved.

A man is his own tormentor and his own condemner. Hence the saying, They shall go into the lake that burns with fire and brimstone. The torment of disappointment in the mind of man is as exquisite as a lake burning with fire and brimstone. I say, so is the torment of man.

I know the scriptures and understand them. I said, no man can commit the unpardonable sin after the dissolution of

---

*Malachi 4:5.

[27]

the body, nor in this life, until he receives the Holy Ghost; but they must do it in this world. Hence the salvation of Jesus Christ was wrought out for all men, in order to triumph over the devil; for if it did not catch him in one place, it would in another; for he stood up. as a Savior. All will suffer until they obey Christ himself.

The contention in heaven was—Jesus said there would be certain souls that would not be saved; and the devil said he could save them all, and laid his plans before the great council, who gave their vote in favor of Jesus Christ. So the devil rose up in rebellion against God, and was cast down, with all who put up their heads for him.*

All sins shall be forgiven, except the sin against the Holy Ghost; for Jesus will save all except the sons of perdition. What must a man do to commit the unpardonable sin? He must receive the Holy Ghost, have the heavens opened unto him, and know God and then sin against him. After a man has sinned against the Holy Ghost, there is no repentance for him.** He has got to say that the sun does not shine while he sees it; he has got to deny Jesus Christ when the heavens have been opened unto him, and to deny the plan of salvation with his eyes open to the truth of it; and from that time he begins to be an enemy. This is the case with many apostates of the Church of Jesus Christ of Latter-day Saints.

When a man begins to be an enemy to this work, he hunts me, he seeks to kill me, and never ceases to thirst for my blood. He gets the spirit of the devil—the same spirit that they had who crucified the Lord of Life—the same spirit that sins against the Holy Ghost. You cannot save such persons; you cannot bring them to repentance; they make open war, like the devil, and awful is the consequence.

---

*Book of Moses (Pearl of Great Price) chapt. 4:1-4; Book of Abraham, chapt. 3:23-28.
**"For it is impossible for those who were once enlightened, and have tasted of the heavenly gift, and were made partakers of the Holy Ghost, and have tasted the good word of God, and the powers of the world to come, if they shall fall away, to renew them again unto repentance; seeing they crucify to themselves the Son of God afresh, and put him to an open shame."—Heb. 4:4-6. Those who sin against the light and knowledge of the Holy Ghost may be said to crucify more than the body of our Lord, they crucify the Spirit.

THE DEGREES OF GLORY

I advise all of you to be careful what you do, or you may by-and-by find out that you have been deceived. Stay yourselves; do not give way; don't make any hasty moves, you may be saved. If a spirit of bitterness is on you, don't be in haste. You may say that man is a sinner. Well, if he repents, he shall be forgiven. Be cautious: await. When you find a spirit that wants bloodshed—murder, the same is not of God, but is of the devil. Out of the abundance of the heart of man the mouth speaketh.

The best men bring forth the best works. The man who tells you words of life is the man who can save you. I warn you against evil characters who sin against the Holy Ghost; for there is no redemption for them in this world nor in the world to come.

I could go back and trace every subject of interest concerning the relationship of man to God, if I had time. I can enter into the mysteries; I can enter largely into the eternal worlds; for Jesus said, "In my Father's house are many mansions; if it were not so, I would have told you. I go to prepare a place for you." (John 14:2). Paul says, "There is one glory of the sun, and another glory of the moon, and another glory of the stars; for one star differeth from another star in glory. So also is the resurrection of the dead" (I Cor. 15:41). What have we to console us in relation to the dead? We have reason to have the greatest hope and consolation for our dead of any people on the earth; for we have seen them walk worthily in our midst, and seen them sink asleep in the arms of Jesus; and those who have died in the faith are now in the celestial kingdom of God. And hence is the glory of the sun.

You mourners have occasion to rejoice, (speaking of the death of Elder King Follett), for your husband and father is gone to wait until the resurrection of the dead—until the perfection of the remainder; for at the resurrection your friend will rise in perfect felicity and go to celestial glory, while many must wait myriads of years before they can receive the like blessings; and your expectations and hopes are far above what man can conceive; for why has God revealed it to us?

I am authorized to say, by the authority of the Holy Ghost,

[29]

that you have no occasion to fear; for he is gone to the home of the just. Don't mourn, don't weep. I know it by the testimony of the Holy Ghost that is within me; and you may wait for your friends to come forth to meet you in the morn of the celestial world.

Rejoice, O Israel! Your friends who have been murdered for the truth's sake in the persecutions shall triumph gloriously in the celestial world, while their murderers shall welter for ages in torment, even until they shall have paid the uttermost farthing. I say this for the benefit of strangers.

I have a father, brothers, children, and friends who have gone to a world of spirits. They are only absent for a moment. They are in the spirit, and we shall meet again. The time will soon arrive when the trumpet shall sound. When we depart, we shall hail our mothers, fathers, friends, and all whom we love, who have fallen. asleep in Jesus. There will be no fear of mobs, persecutions or malicious lawsuits and arrests; but it will be an eternity of felicity.

I will leave this subject here, and make a few remarks on the subject of baptism. The baptism of water, without the baptism of fire and the Holy Ghost attending it, is of no use; they are necessarily and inseparably connected. An individual must be born of water and the spirit in order to get into the kingdom of God. In the German, the text bears me out the same as the revelations which I have given and taught for the last fourteen years on that subject. I have the testimony to put in their teeth. My testimony has been true all the time. You will find it in the declaration of John the Baptist. (Reads from the German.) John says "I baptize you with water, but when Jesus comes, who has the power (or keys), he shall administer the baptism of fire and the Holy Ghost." Great God! where is now all the sectarian world? And if this testimony is true, they are all damned as clearly as anathema can do it. I know the text is true. I call upon all you Germans, who know that it is true, to say, Aye (Loud shouts of "Aye.")

Alexander Campbell, how are you going to save people with water alone? For John said his baptism was good for nothing without the baptism of Jesus Christ. "Therefore, *not* leaving

[30]

the principles of the doctrine of Christ, let us go on unto perfection; not laying again the foundation of repentance from dead works, and of faith toward God, and of the doctrine of baptisms, and of laying on of hands, and of resurrection of the dead and of eternal judgment. And this will we do, if God permit." (Heb. 6:1-3).* * *

Hear it, all ye ends of the earth—all ye priests, all ye sinners, and all men. Repent! repent! Obey the gospel. Turn to God; for your religion won't save you, and you will be damned. I do not say how long. There have been remarks made concerning all men being redeemed from hell; but I say that those who sin against the Holy Ghost cannot be forgiven in this world or in the world to come; they shall die the second death. Those who commit the unpardonable sin are doomed to *Gnolom*—to dwell in hell, worlds without end. As they concoct scenes of bloodshed in this world, so they shall rise to that resurrection which is as the lake of fire and brimstone. Some shall rise to the everlasting burnings of God; for God dwells in everlasting burnings, and some shall rise to the damnation of their own filthiness, which is as exquisite a torment as the lake of fire and brimstone.

I have intended my remarks for all, both rich and poor, bond and free, great and small. I have no enmity against any man. I love you all; but I hate some of your deeds. I am your best friend, and if persons miss their mark it is their own fault. If I reprove a man, and he hates me, he is a fool; for I love all men, especially these my brethren and sisters.

I rejoice in hearing the testimony of my aged friends. You don't know me; you never knew my heart. No man knows my history. I cannot tell it; I shall never undertake it. I don't blame any one for not believing my history; if I had not experienced what I have I could not have believed it myself. I never did harm any man since I was born in the world. My voice is always for peace.

I cannot lie down until all my work is finished. I never think any evil, nor do anything to the harm of my fellow-man. When I am called by the trump of the arch-angel and weighed in the balance, you will all know me then. I add no more. God bless you all. Amen.

THE VISION

THE THREE GLORIES

By President Brigham Young

(Remarks made in the Bowery, Great Salt Lake City, August 26, 1860.)

"I will read a portion of the vision Joseph Smith and Sidney Rigdon had concerning various kingdoms that God has prepared for his subjects: (See Sec. 92:7 Doc. and Cov., the then current edition—1860. Now Sec. 76:96-113.)

"I do not know that I have any particular desire to dwell upon this any more than any other subject of the Gospel, although this subject, in the abstract, occupies more of my affection, adoration, and heartfelt gratitude to our Father and God than any other that has ever been revealed to my knowledge, from the days of Adam to the present.

"Looking at the human family—the millions of intelligent beings who have come upon this earth from the days of Adam until now, and those that must still come in the course of events —the question naturally arises, What are they created for? what is the object of their being? None of them have power to produce themselves. Jesus Christ is the heir of this vast family. He said that he had power to lay down his life and take it up again; but he had no more power to produce his life, in the beginning of his existence, than we have. Every human being is endowed, more or less, with eternal intelligence, with the germ of life everlasting, of glory immortal; and then, when I view the human family as they are, with the traditions of the fathers, what the Bible has taught, what the priests have taught, and what kings and rulers have introduced and fastened upon their people, through traditions and customs, and contemplate the variety now existing and that has existed upon the earth, the marks of these finites, and what is their end, I can truly say that, in my estimation, no other revelation so glorious was ever given. You may read the character of the Deity as portrayed in all that has ever been revealed, until you come to this vision, in relation to his justice, his judgment, his power, his life, his glory, his excellence, his goodness, his mercy, and the fullness of every gift, of every trait, of every principle inherent in the

[32]

character of the Supreme Being, and it is not equal in magnitude, in my reflections, to that which God revealed to Joseph Smith and Sidney Rigdon in the vision from which I have read.

"We are far advanced in the things of the kingdom of God. To say nothing about any other principle or doctrine that has ever been revealed, the transcending glory, excellency, wisdom, goodness, virtue, and power that God has revealed in this vision far outweigh all the Christian tenets, doctrines, and systems they have drawn from the Bible. No cistern, to use a figure, hewn by man, can hold water; and every human doctrine and principle, professing to point the way of salvation, fades away. The doctrine God has revealed here is more precious to me, and is worth more than all the doctrines of Christendom.

"We may read that the Lord will turn the wicked into hell, and all the nations that forget God; but, so far as the Bible and priests are concerned, the world is left in the dark upon what this vision reveals. Fatality is sealed on the world by the priests as an everlasting inheritance and legacy, from which they never can be delivered. Their doom is to dwell in a lake of fire and brimstone. God has created this intelligence to preserve it. If the world, with its present feelings, believed this vision, they would say—'Our condition will be so far better than we had anticipated, that we will continue our course; for we love the world and the things of the world, and we will roll sin as a sweet morsel under our tongues, and delight in all the iniquity we have indulged in from youth, and continue to imbibe the erroneous principles taught by the fathers and others, and will pass on from day to day; for our condition is to be so far better than our priests have taught us.' It would have been better for them had they never been born, were it not so.

"Were the wicked, in their sins, under the necessity of walking into the presence of the Father and Son, hand-in-hand with those who believe that all will be saved—that Jesus will leave none, their condition would be more excruciating and unendurable than to dwell in the lake that burns with fire and brimstone. The fatalist's doctrine consigns to hell the infant not a span long, while the adulterer, whoremonger, thief, liar, false swearer, murderer, and every other abominable character, if they but repent on the gallows or their death-beds, are, by the same doctrine, forced into the presence of the Father and the Son, which, could they enter there, would be a hell to them.

"The kingdoms that God has prepared are innumerable. Each and every intelligent being will be judged according to the deeds done in the body, according to his works, faith, desires, and honesty or dishonesty before God; every trait of his character will receive its just merit or demerit, and he will be judged according to the law of heaven as revealed; and God has prepared places suited to every class. The Saviour said to his disciples—'In my Father's house are many mansions: if it were not so I would have told you. I go to prepare a place for you. And if I go and prepare a place for you, I will come again and receive you unto myself, that where I am, there ye may be also.' How many kingdoms there are has not been told to us: they are innumerable. The disciples of Jesus were to dwell with him. Where will the rest go? Into kingdoms prepared for them, where they will live and endure. Jesus will bring forth, by his own redemption, every son and daughter of Adam, except the sons of perdition, who will be cast into hell. Others will suffer the wrath of God—will suffer all the Lord can demand at their hands, or justice can require of them; and when they have suffered the wrath of God till the utmost farthing is paid, they will be brought out of prison. Is this dangerous doctrine to preach? Some consider it dangerous; but it is true that every person who does not sin away the day of grace, and become an angel to the Devil will be brought forth to inherit a kingdom of glory.

"The sectarian world, as we call them, is a professed church of God without the Priesthood. Sectarians have not the Priesthood; but all of them who live according to the best light and intelligence they can obtain through faithfulness to what they believe, as taught unto them, will receive a kingdom and glory that will far transcend all their expectations, imaginations, or visions in their most excited moments, whether in their falling-down power, jumping power, or squawling power. All they have ever desired or anticipated they will receive, and far more; but they cannot dwell with the Father and Son, unless they go through these ordeals that are ordained for the Church of the First born. The ordinances of the house of God are expressly for the Church of the First born.

" 'Go into all the world and preach the gospel to every creature. He that believeth and is baptized shall be saved, and he that believeth not shall be damned; and these signs shall follow them that believe. In my name, etc.' This is the law of the celestial kingdom, and those who hearken to this law, and embrace its truths in their faith, and live them in their lives, will be brought to enjoy the presence of the Son, and will dwell with him and the Father. And all the residue, who do not sin against the Holy Ghost, will be punished according to their deeds, and will receive according to their works, whether it be little or much, good or bad. Jesus will redeem the last and least of the sons of Adam, except the sons of perdition, who will be held in reserve for another time. They will become angels of the Devil.

"What say you, ye Latter-day Saints? Is not this the most glorious thought that ever was revealed to mortal man? Let the Elders of this Church go forth and preach that every person who does not become as they are will have to suffer the wrath of God and go down to hell to dwell in a lake that burns with brimstone and fire, 'Where the worm dieth not and the fire is not quenched,' and I would not give the ashes of a rye-straw for all they will do. It is good for nothing: there is no life in it —there is no soul in it.

"This intelligence must endure. We must preserve our identity before the Lord, who has sent his Son and angels, and is sending the Holy Ghost, and his ministers, and revelations, to comfort, cheer, guide, and direct the affairs of his kingdom on the earth. Shall we dwindle out in our faith, and in those blessings God bestows on us at this time? No. Let us live to increase them. Let us so live, that when we receive our bodies in the resurrection, we will be received in the presence of the Father and the Son. This kingdom is designed expressly to prepare the people to dwell with God the Father and his Son Jesus Christ, and all the world beside will receive according to their works upon the earth. This is a joy that is unspeakable: it is a glory beyond the capacity of our minds at the present time to appreciate. It is a great joy to me.

"Sometimes I feel as though I would like to dwell upon these principles, they are so delightful; but I do not feel like preaching or talking much this morning. The glory and intelligence that God has prepared for the faithful, and for every other being that is worthy to receive, expand, extend, and comprehend, no man knoweth. Should not this fill every heart with peace and joy—that there is no end to the progress of knowledge? Let us continue to prepare ourselves to dwell with Him in eternal burnings. May the Lord bless the people. Amen."

Journal of Discourses, Vol. 8, pp. 152-5.

ളം

THE THREE GLORIES

By Elder Orson Pratt

"What subject I may present before you tonight I do not know. Sometimes a subject will open to my mind while I am listening to the singers, and sometimes I rise without having the first thing before my mind to speak to the people, and I trust in God to give me what is needful at the very moment. This is the case with me this evening, and I do humbly pray to my Father in heaven, in the name of his beloved Son, that he will grant unto me the Spirit to discern what to say and what would be most adapted to the wants of those who are present. There is such a vast field of light and truth which God has revealed in different ages of the world, and more especially in our times, that the great difficulty with the servant of God, I have often thought is to distinguish and discern what portion of the great variety would be most pleasing in the sight of the Lord to lay before the people." * * *

"As we have not time to enter fully into the investigation of all these different glories, I wish more particularly to inquire concerning the nature of this higher state of glory called celestial. Will there be any difference among those who are redeemed into that glory? There will, in some respects. They will all be equal in the enjoyment of some blessings, and so far their glory will be the same, but yet in some respects there will be a difference. Some who will inherit a portion of that glory will have no families, they will be deprived of that blessing to all ages of eternity, while others will receive an exaltation and kingdom, and will have wives, children, dominion, greatness and power far above those I first referred to.

"Now why should there be this distinction in the celestial kingdom, and what is the cause of it? It is because certain persons who have obeyed the Gospel have become careless and indifferent in regard to securing that high exaltation which was within their reach. God has revealed to this people what is needful for an exaltation in his kingdom. He has revealed to us, as we heard from Elder Hyde this afternoon, that marriage is destined for eternity as well as time—that the marriage covenant between male and female must be entered into in this life and the ordinance performed here by those whom God has appointed and ordained to hold the keys and authority to seal on earth that it may be sealed in heaven; for in heaven there is neither marrying nor giving in marriage; no such thing can be attended to there. Now persons among the Latter-day Saints who do not enter into this covenant of marriage but prefer to lead a single life cannot enjoy all that fullness of exaltation which will be possessed by those who have had this covenant sealed upon them. They might not have forfeited the blessing of the celestial glory altogether, but they have forfeited the right to have wives by which only they could have a posterity in the eternal worlds. Who will be the subjects in the kingdom which they will rule who are exalted in the celestial kingdom of our God? Will they reign over their neighbors' children? Oh, no. Over whom, then, will they reign? Their own children, their own posterity will be the citizens of their kingdoms; in other words, the patriarchal order will prevail there to the endless ages of eternity, and the children of each patriarch will be his while eternal ages roll on. This is not according to present customs, for now when a young man reaches the age of twenty-one years he is free from his parents, and considers that he is no longer under the necessity of being controlled by his father. That is according to our customs, and the laws of our country. It is a very good law and adapted to the imperfections that now exist; but it will not be so in the eternal worlds. There will never be any such thing there as being from under their father's rule, no matter whether twenty-one or twenty-one thousand years of age, it will make no difference, they will still be subject to the laws of their Patriarch or Father, and they must observe and obey them throughout all eternity. There is only one way by which children can be freed from that celestial law and order of things, and that is by rebellion. They are agents, and they can rebel against God and against the order of things he has instituted there, just as Satan and the fallen angels rebelled and turned away. The increase of those who are exalted in that kingdom will endure for ever; and the bringing forth of children will not be attended with sorrow, pain and distress as it is here; these evils have come in consequence of the fall of man and the transgression by him of God's holy laws. But when men are redeemed to immortality and eternal life there will be no pain, sorrow or affliction of body, and yet children will be brought forth, and to their increase there will be no end. Hence the promise of God to the patriarchs Abraham, Isaac and Jacob, that their seed should be as numerous as the stars of heaven, or as the sands upon the sea shore. We all know that the sand on the sea shore is innumerable to us. If we take a handful it numbers tens of thousands of grains, and if Abraham's seed are to become as numerous as the sands on the sea shore they will fill a great many worlds like this of ours. There is to be no end to the increase of the old Patriarch, and, as his posterity increases, world on world will be created, and brought into existence, and those children will be sent forth from the presence of the Patriarch to take upon themselves bodies, as we have done here in this world. I mean their spirits. Understand me now, resurrected parents are the parents not of bodies of flesh and bones, but of spirits the same as we were before we came and took these mortal bodies, that

[38]

is, when we lived up in yonder world in the presence of our Father, and in the company of the thousands of millions of our brother and sister spirits. They will be of the same class and nature, and they will have to take their positions in worlds that will be created for them the same as we came from heaven to this world, that we might gain knowledge and experience that we could not gain in any other way. Thus will the Lord continue his work and purposes, and there will be one eternal round in creation, and redemption, in the formation and re-demption of worlds, and bringing them back into his presence.

"We read that God is the Father of our spirits, the Father of the spirits of all flesh Moses calls him. The Apostle Paul tells the Saints in his day that we have fathers in the flesh who have corrected us, how much more ought we to be obedient to the Father of our spirits and live?

"What will become of the old bachelor who refuses to obey the ordinance of marriage? We have preached to the young men of this Territory, and laid before them the sacred-ness of the marriage covenant. We have told them and the young women that it is their duty to enter into this covenant as much as it is their duty to be baptized for the remission of their sins. The God that commanded the latter gave the revelation concerning the marriage covenant, yet there are some who will give heed to one ordinance, baptism, but will be careless and indifferent about the other. By taking this course they do not altogether forfeit their right and title to enter that kingdom, but they do forfeit their right and title to be kings therein. What will be their condition there? They will be angels.

"There are many different classes of beings in the eternal worlds, and among them are angels. Who are these angels? Some of them have never yet come to take upon them bodies of flesh and bones, but they will come in their times, seasons and generations and receive their tabernacles the same as we have done. Then there are others who were resurrected when Jesus was, when the graves of the Saints were opened and many came forth and showed themselves to those who were then living in the flesh. Besides these there are angels who have

[39]

been to this world and have never yet received a resurrection, whose spirits have gone hence into celestial paradise, and there await the resurrection. We have now mentioned three classes of angels. There are others, among them some redeemed from former creations before this world was made, one of whom administered to our first parents after they were cast out of the garden as they were offering sacrifices and burnt offerings, according to the commandments which they received from God when they were driven from the garden. After they had done this many days an angel came and ministered to them and inquired of them why they offered sacrifices and burnt offerings unto the Lord. The answer was, 'I know not, save the Lord commanded me.' Then this angel went on to explain to our first parents why these offerings were made and why they were commanded to shed the blood of beasts, telling them that all these things were typical of the great and last sacrifice that should be offered up for *all* mankind, namely, the Son of the living God. These angels that came to Adam were not men who had been redeemed from this earth—not men who had been translated from this earth—but they pertained to former worlds. They understood about the coming of Jesus, the nature of these sacrifices, etc.

"Some of these angels have received their exaltation, and still are called angels. For instance, Michael has received his exaltation. He is not without his kingdom and crown, wife or wives and posterity, because he lived faithful to the end. Who is he? Our first great progenitor, Adam, is called Michael, the Prince. I am mentioning now things that the Latter-day Saints are acquainted with. Many of these things I have just been quoting are revelations given to us, as those who are readers will recollect. Some of these angels have received their exaltation. They are kings, they are priests, they have entered into their glory and sit upon thrones—they hold the sceptre over their posterity. Those other classes I have mentioned have neglected the new and everlasting covenant of marriage: They can not inherit this glory and these kingdoms—they can not be crowned in the celestial world. What purpose will they serve? They will be sent on errands—be sent to other worlds as missionaries, to minister. They will be sent on whatever business the Lord sees proper. In other words, they will be servants. To whom will they be servants? To those who have obeyed and remained faithful to the new and everlasting covenant, and have been exalted to thrones; to those who have covenanted before God with wives so that they may raise up and multiply immortal intelligent beings through all the ages of eternity. Here is the distinction of classes, but all of the same glory, called celestial glory.

"But how about these terrestrials, can they come up into the celestial? No, their intelligence and knowledge have not prepared and adapted them to dwell with those who reign in celestial glory, consequently they can not even be angels in that glory. They have not obeyed the law that pertains to that glory, and hence they could not abide it. But will there be blessings administered to them by those who dwell in celestial glory? Yes, angels will be sent forth from the celestial world to minister to those who inherit the glory of the moon, bearing messages of joy and peace and of all that which is calculated to exalt, to redeem and ennoble those who have been resurrected into a terrestrial glory. They can receive the Spirit of the Lord there, and the ministration of angels there.

"Now let us come to still inferior glories. I have mentioned those who inherit the glory of the stars. Who are they? They are not the heathen, for they come up higher—into the terrestrial glory. Who are they, then, who are permitted only to inherit a glory typified by the stars? They are the general world of mankind, those who have heard the Gospel of the Son of God but have not obeyed it. They are to be punished. How long? Until Jesus has reigned here on the earth a thousand years. How much longer? Until the 'little season' has passed away after the end of the thousand years, and then when the final end shall come and the trump of God shall sound, and the great white throne shall appear and the heaven and the earth shall flee away; when that time shall come, the sound of the trump shall call forth those sleeping millions of all ages, generations and nations who have heard the sound of the

Gospel and have not obeyed it, but until then their bodies must sleep. They are not worthy of the first resurrection. 'Blessed and holy is he who has part in the first resurrection, for on such the second death has no power.' But those who will not give heed to the law of the Gospel have no claim on this first resurrection, and their bodies must sleep through all these long centuries that are to intervene between the time of their death and the end of the earth. Where will their spirits be all that time? Not in any glory; they cannot inherit a glory until their punishment is past. They are not permitted to enter into prison. A great many people, and perhaps some of the Latter-day Saints, have supposed that these characters will go into prison. I do not know of any revelation anywhere intimating that any one of this class of persons will ever be put *in* prison. Where do they go? To another place altogether different from a prison. A prison is designed for those *who* never heard the Gospel here in the flesh, but yet have committed a few sins without the knowledge of the revealed law, and who have to be beaten with few stripes in prison. But those persons who hear the Gospel, as the nations of the present dispensation are doing, can not go to prison, it is not their place. They fall below a prison, into outer darkness or hell, where there will be weeping and wailing and gnashing of teeth. There they have to remain with the devil and his angels in torment and misery until the final end, then they come forth. Can they come where God and Christ dwell? No, worlds without end they cannot come there. Can they go into the presence of the heathen where the glory is that of the moon? No, they cannot even come there. When they are delivered from the power of Satan and endless death and brought forth, where do they go? If they do not go into the presence of God the Father, if they are not counted worthy to enter into the terrestrial world among the heathen, where will they go? God has provided mansions for them according to their works here in this world. Having suffered the vengeance of eternal fire for the space of a thousand years and upwards, and suffered the extreme penalty of the law of God, they can now be brought forth to inherit a

[42]

place where they can be administered unto by terrestrial beings and by Angels holding the Priesthood, and where they can receive the Holy Ghost.

"Those in the terrestrial world have the privilege of beholding Jesus sometimes—they can receive the presence of the Son, but not of the fullness of the Father; but those in the telestial world, still lower, receive only the Holy Ghost, administered to them by messengers ordained and sent forth to minister to them for glory and exaltation, providing they will obey the law that is given unto them, which law will be telestial law. That will finally exalt them. How far I know not, but where God and Christ are they can not come, worlds without end.

"Now I think I have set forth these glories and these different degrees of punishment, and the different classes of people that are to be judged according to the knowledge that they have here in this world. I have set these things forth as plainly as I am capable of doing in one short discourse; and will bring my remarks to a close in a few moments.

"We are what the Lord calls Latter-day Saints—we have received light and knowledge to that degree from the heavens that will, if obeyed, exalt us to these high privileges of which I have been speaking. On the other hand, if not obeyed, that very light and knowledge are sufficient to sink us below all things. Hence we stand on dangerous ground in some respects, and we have need to fear lest we sin against this light and have not the privilege of even the telestial world. He that rejects this covenant (let me quote the word of the Lord given in these last days)—'He that rejecteth this covenant and altogether turns therefrom, shall not have forgiveness of sins in this world nor in the world to come.' Do you hear it, Latter-day Saints? If you do, then strive with all your hearts to be faithful. Strive to abide in the covenant that you have received. There is no halfway business with us—we have got to remain faithful to this covenant, for if we turn away from it we can not even claim the glory that the world will have when the last resurrection shall come, but our doom is fixed—we have to dwell with the devil and his angels to all eternity.

Why? Because they once had light and knowledge, dwelt in the presence of God, and knew about the glories of His kingdom. But they rebelled, and kept not the law that was given to them—they sinned against light and knowledge and were thrust down in chains of darkness, there to remain until the judgment of the great day. If we do not wish to be placed in their society for all eternity we must abide in the covenant that we have made. If we do this, Latter-day Saints, glory and honor and immortality and eternal lives, and thrones and kingdoms and dominions and creations and worlds will be given to us, and our posterity will increase until, like the sand on the sea shore, they cannot be numbered. Amen."

(Excerpts from discourse delivered in the 14th Ward Assembly Rooms, Salt Lake City, Sunday evening, January 19, 1873)

Journal of Discourses, Vol. 15, pp. 319-324.

THE THREE GLORIES

(Excerpts from sermon delivered by Elder Melvin J. Ballard in the Ogden Tabernacle, Ogden, on September 22, 1922)

By Permission

"I now say to all the world that no man, or woman, ever shall see the Celestial Kingdom of God who is not baptized of the water and of the spirit. The Lord has specified it. He made it so binding and complete when after announcing the law he complied with every term himself, though perfect, so that no man who imagines himself to be perfect here can excuse himself or herself from obedience to the law of baptism. It is the door, the gate to Celestial Glory.

"'That by keeping the commandments they might be washed and cleansed from all their sins, and receive the Holy Spirit by the laying on of the hands of him who is ordained and sealed unto this power.'

"'And who overcome by faith, and are sealed by the Holy Spirit of promise, which the Father sheds forth upon all those who are just and true.'

[44]

THE DEGREES OF GLORY

"I would like to pause and emphasize that passage, because, while we receive eternal blessings at the hands of the priesthood which has the right to seal on earth and it shall be sealed in Heaven, this revelation clearly states it must be sealed by the Holy Spirit of promise also.

"A man and woman may by fraud and deception obtain admittance to the house of the Lord and may receive the pronouncement of the holy priesthood, giving to them, so far as lies in their power, these blessings. We may deceive men but we cannot deceive the Holy Ghost, and our blessings will not be eternal unless they are also sealed by the Holy Spirit of promise, the Holy Ghost, one who reads the thoughts and hearts of men and gives his sealing approval to the blessings pronounced upon their heads. Then it is binding, efficacious and of full force.

"I thank the Lord that there is this provision, so that even though men are able to deceive their brethren, they are not able to deceive the Holy Ghost and thus come into possession of their blessings unless they prove in word, in thought, and in deed their worthiness and righteousness.

* * * *

"Now, I would like to say a word or two about that Mormon truism, namely: 'As man is God once was, and as God is man may become.'

"Note that it is not to the effect that man will become, but man may become, and I wish to say that few men will become what God is. And yet, all men may become what He is if they will pay the price.

"Now, I wish to say to you that the only possible candidates to become what God is are those who attain Celestial Glory, and those who fail in that will never, worlds without end, be possible candidates to become what God is. Then I wish to say to you that there are three degrees of glory in the Celestial Kingdom and only those who attain the highest degree of Celestial Glory will be candidates to become what God is.

"So you see, it is within the reach of every man and woman who lives, but only attainable by those who pay the price, who stand the test, who prove themselves, who comply with the terms and conditions that make their calling and election sure.

* * * *

"A man may receive the priesthood and all its privileges and blessings, but until he learns to overcome the flesh, his temper, his tongue, his disposition to indulge in the things God has forbidden, he cannot come into the Celestial Kingdom of God—he must overcome either in this life or in the life to come. But this life is the time in which men are to repent. Do not let any of us imagine that we can go down to the grave not having overcome the corruptions of the flesh and then lose in the grave all our sins and evil tendencies. They will be with us. They will be with the spirit when separated from the body.

"It is my judgment that any man or woman can do more to conform to the laws of God in one year in this life than they could in ten years when they are dead. The spirit only can repent and change, and then the battle has to go forward with the flesh afterwards. It is much easier to overcome and serve the Lord when both flesh and spirit are combined as one. This is the time when men are more pliable and susceptible. We will find when we are dead every desire, every feeling will be greatly intensified. When clay is pliable it is much easier to change than when it gets hard and sets.

"This life is the time to repent. That is why I presume it will take a thousand years after the first resurrection until the last group will be prepared to come forth. It will take them a thousand years to do what it would have taken, but three score years to accomplish in this life.

"You remember the vision of the redemption of the dead as given to the Church through the late President Joseph F. Smith. President Smith saw the spirits of the righteous dead before their resurrection and the language is the same as one of the Prophet Joseph's revelations—that they, the righteous dead, looked upon the absence of their spirits from their bodies as a bondage.

"I grant you that the righteous dead will be at peace, but I tell you that when we go out of this life, leave this body, we will desire to do many things that we cannot do at all without

[46]

the body. We will be seriously handicapped, and we will long for the body; we will pray for that early reunion with our bodies. We will know then what advantage it is to have a body.

"Then, every man and woman who is putting off until the next life the task of correcting and overcoming the weakness of the flesh are sentencing themeslves to years of bondage, for no man or woman will come forth in the resurrection until they have completed their work, until they have overcome, until they have done as much as they can do. That is why Jesus said in the resurrection there is neither marriage or giving in marriage, for all such contracts—agreements—will be provided for those who are worthy of it before men and women come forth in the resurrection, and those who are complying in this life with these conditions are shortening their sentences, for every one of us will have a matter of years in that spirit state to complete and finish our salvation. And some may attain, by reason of their righteousness in this life, the right to do postgraduate work, to be admitted into the Celestial Kingdom, but others will lose absolutely the right to that glory, all they can do will not avail after death to bring them into the Celestial Kingdom.

* * * *

"Some folks get the notion that the problems of life will at once clear up and they will know that this is the Gospel of Christ when they die. I have heard people say they believe when they die they will see Peter and that he will clear it all up. I said, 'You never will see Peter until you accept the Gospel of the Lord Jesus Christ, at the hands of the elders of the Church, living or dead.' They will meet these men to whom this right and authority has been given, for this generation shall receive it at the hands of those who have been honored with the priesthood of this dispensation. Living or dead, they shall not hear it from anyone else.

"So, men won't know any more when they are dead than when they are living, only they will have passed through the change called death. They will not understand the truths of the Gospel only by the same process as they understand and comprehend them here. So when they hear the Gospel preached in the spirit world they will respond just as our fathers and mothers have, with a glad heart. They will love it and embrace it. It will then be easy to know who they are. They who have died without the knowledge of the truth, they who will receive it with glad hearts, they also will be candidates for Celestial Glory. When you die and go to the spirit world you will labor for years, trying to convert individuals who will be taking their own course. Some of them will repent; some of them will listen. Another group will be rebellious, following their own will and notion, and that group will get smaller and smaller until every knee shall humbly bow and every tongue confess.

"It may take us thousands of years to do that. But those who are of the blood of Israel, who, had they been living, would have received the Gospel and are not participators in the blessings, will in a similar manner receive it in the spirit world.

* * * *

"Now I wish to answer one or two queries that undoubtedly have arisen in your minds, and in doing so I wish to read some more scripture. The question is often asked, 'Is it possible for one who attains Telestial Glory in time in the eternal world to live so well that he may graduate from the Telestial and pass into the Terrestrial, and then after a season that he may progress from that and be ultimately worthy of the Celestial Glory?' That is the query that has been asked. I have just read the answer, so far as the Telestial group is concerned. 'Where God and Christ dwell they cannot come, worlds without end.' I take it upon the same basis, the same argument likewise applies to the Terrestrial World. Those whose lives have entitled them to Terrestrial Glory can never gain Celestial Glory. One who gains possession of the lowest degree of the Telestial Glory may ultimately arise to the highest degree of that glory, but no provision has been made for promotion from one glory to another. Let us be reasonable about it.

"I wish to say in illustrating the subject that if three men were starting out on an endless race, one having an advantage of one mile, the other of two miles, and each one could run as fast as the other, when would the last ever catch up to the first? If you can tell me that, I can tell you when candidates for the Telestial Glory will get into the Celestial Glory. Each will grow, but their development will be prescribed by their environment, and there is a reason for it.

"Applying this illustration to those who are entitled to the different degrees of glory: He who enters the Celestial Glory has the advantage over all others. He dwells in the presence of the Father and the Son. His teachers are the highest. The others will receive all they learn from the Celestial to the Terrestrial, from the Terrestrial to the Telestial. They get it second hand and third hand, and how can they ever hope to grow as fast as those who drink from the fountain head. Again, those who come forth in the Celestial Glory with Celestial bodies have bodies that are more refined. They are different. The very fibre and texture of the Celestial body is more pure and holy than a Telestial or Terrestrial body, and a Celestial body alone can endure Celestial Glory. I am impressed with this because I recall when a child at school I learned that if an icicle a mile square were dropped into the sun it would melt in an instant, and when I learned how intense the heat of that orb is and that our sun is a Celestial world, I did not know whether I wanted to live in a Celestial world or not if it was that hot. But when I come to understand, if I have a body suitable to dwell in eternal burnings then I think I would like it. Fishes can live in the water and have bodies suited to that element but entirely unsuitable to a life outside of the water. When we have a Celestial body it will be suited to the Celestial conditions and a Telestial body could not endure Celestial Glory. It would be torment and affliction to them. I have not read in the scripture where there will be another resurrection where we can obtain a Celestial body for a Terrestrial body. What we receive in the resurrection will be ours forever and forever.

"I have several times been asked, how is it possible for those who attain Celestial glory to ever feel happy and satisfied to know that their children are in the Telestial world, and never would have the privilege of coming up with their parents in the Celestial Kingdom.

"We must not overlook the fact that those who attain to the higher glories may minister unto and visit and associate with those of the lesser kingdoms. While the lesser may not come up, they may still enjoy the companionship of their loved ones who are in higher stations. Also we must not forget that even the least degree of glory, as the Lord has expressed it, is beyond all our present understanding. So that they are in the presence of glorious conditions, even though they attain unto the least place, and we must not forget either that these are our Father's sons and daughters, and he has other sons and daughters who do not even attain unto the Telestial Kingdom. They are sons of perdition out with the devil and his angels and though the Father has grieved over them, He still has not the power to rescue and save them because He gave them free agency and they used that in such a manner that they have shut themselves out from His presence. But He is justified. He has performed His full duty by them and that is the condition which we ought to be in to feel justified, though we may be so unfortunate as to have some of our own children in the lesser kingdoms, if we have done our full duty by them, we may be sad at the thought of their not being with us, but we will not have the sting or remorse of conscience. If we have failed, however, to do our duty, then naturally we feel to regret their situation and censure ourselves in part for the same."

~

THE FORE-KNOWLEDGE OF THE GREAT JEHOVAH

By JOSEPH THE PROPHET

"The great Jehovah contemplated the whole of the events connected with the earth, pertaining to the plan of salvation, before it rolled into existence, or ever 'the morning stars sang together' for joy; the past, the present, and the future were and

are, with Him, one eternal 'now;' He knew of the fall of
Adam, the iniquities of the antediluvians, of the depth of iniquity that would be connected with the human family, their
weaknesses and strength, their power and glory, apostasies, their
crimes, their righteousness and iniquity; He comprehended the
fall of man, and his redemption; He knew the plan of salvation
and pointed it out; He was acquainted with the situation of
all nations and with their destiny; He ordered all things according to the council of His own will; He knows the situation of
both the living and the dead, and has made ample provision
for their redemption, according to their several circumstances,
and the laws of the kingdom of God, whether in this world, or
in the world to come."

D. H. C., Vol. 4, p. 597.

ॐ

THE REDEMPTION OF THE DEAD

By Joseph the Prophet

"And now, my dearly beloved brethren and sisters, let
me assure you that these are principles in relation to the dead
and the living that cannot be lightly passed over, as pertaining
to our salvation. For their salvation is necessary and essential
to our salvation, as Paul says concerning the fathers, that they
without us cannot be made perfect, neither can we without our
dead be made perfect.

"And now, in relation to the baptism for the dead, I will
give you another quotation of Paul, I Corinthians 15:29: 'Else
what shall they do which are baptized for the dead, if the dead
rise not at all? Why are they then baptized for the dead?'

"And again, in connection with this quotation I will give
you a quotation from one of the prophets, who had his eye
fixed on the restoration of the priesthood, the glories to be
revealed in the last days, and in an especial manner this most
glorious of all subjects belonging to the everlasting gospel,
namely, the baptism for the dead; for Malachi says, last chap-

ter, verses 5th and 6th: 'Behold, I will send you Elijah the prophet before the coming of the great and dreadful day of the Lord; And he shall turn the heart of the fathers to the children, and the heart of the children to their fathers, lest I come and smite the earth with a curse.'

"I might have rendered a plainer translation to this, but it is sufficiently plain to suit my purpose as it stands. It is sufficient to know, in this case, that the earth will be smitten with a curse unless there is a welding link of some kind or other between the fathers and the children, upon some subject or other and behold what is that subject? It is the baptism for the dead. For we without them cannot be made perfect; neither can they without us be made perfect. Neither can they nor we be made perfect without those who have died in the gospel also; for it is necessary in the ushering in of the dispensation of the fulness of times, which dispensation is now beginning to usher in, that a whole and complete and perfect union, and welding together of dispensations, and keys, and powers, and glories should take place, and be revealed from the days of Adam even to the present time. And not only this, but those things which never have been revealed from the foundation of the world, but have been kept hid from the wise and prudent, shall be revealed unto babes and sucklings in this, the dispensation of the fulness of times."

Doc. and Cov., Section 128:15-18.

THE EFFICACY OF THE SEALING ORDINANCE

By JOSEPH THE PROPHET

"Four destroying angels holding power over the four quarters of the earth until the servants of God are sealed in their foreheads, which signifies sealing the blessing upon their heads, meaning the everlasting covenant, thereby making their calling and election sure. *When a seal is put upon the father and mother, it secures their posterity, so that they cannot be lost,*

but will be saved by virtue of the covenant of their father and mother."
(*Remarks delivered at the funeral of Judge Higbee on Sunday, August 13, 1843*)
Historical Record, p. 531.

ॐ

THE SEALING POWER OF MINISTERING SPIRITS

By Joseph the Prophet

"All men know that they must die. And it is important that we should understand the reasons and causes of our exposure to the vicissitudes of life and of death, and the designs and purposes of God in our coming into the world, our sufferings here, and our departure hence. Could you gaze into heaven five minutes, you would know more than you would by reading all that was ever written on the subject. * * *

"The organization of the spiritual and heavenly worlds, and of spiritual and heavenly beings, was agreeable to the most perfect order and harmony: their limits and bounds were fixed irrevocably, and voluntarily subscribed to in their heavenly estate by themselves, and were by our first parents subscribed to upon the earth. Hence the importance of embracing and subscribing to principles of eternal truth by all men upon the earth that expect eternal life. * * *

"Spirits can only be revealed in flaming fire or glory. Angels have advanced further, their light and glory being tabernacled; and hence they appear in bodily shape. *The spirits of just men are made ministering servants to those who are sealed unto life eternal, and it is through them that the sealing power comes down.* * * *

"Angels have advanced higher in knowledge and power than spirits. * * * *The spirits of the just are elevated to a greater and more glorious work; hence they are blessed in their departure to the world of spirits. Enveloped in flaming fire, they are not far from us, and know and understand our*

[53]

thoughts, feelings and emotions, and are often pained therewith.
"Flesh and blood cannot go there; but flesh and bones, quickened by the Spirit of God, can."
(Remarks delivered at the funeral of General Adams,
October 9, 1843)
Historical Record, p. 533.

ൠ

PREACHING TO SPIRITS IN PRISON

By PRESIDENT BRIGHAM YOUNG

"Jesus had a work to do on the earth. He performed his mission, and then was slain for his testimony. So it has been with every man who has been foreordained to perform certain important missions. Joseph Smith truly said: 'No power can take away my life until my work is done.' All the powers of earth and hell could not take his life, until he had completed the work the Father gave him to do; until that was done he had to live. When he died he had a mission in the spirit world, as much so as Jesus had. Jesus was the first man that ever went to preach to the spirits in prison, holding the keys of the gospel of salvation to them. Those keys were delivered to him in the day and hour that he went into the spirit world, and with them he opened the door of salvation to the spirits in prison.

"Compare those inhabitants on the earth who have heard the Gospel in our day, with the millions who have never heard it, or had the keys of salvation presented to them, and you will conclude at once as I do, that there is an almighty work to perform in the spirit world. Joseph has not yet got through there. When he finishes his mission in the spirit world, he will be resurrected, but he has not yet done there. Reflect upon the millions and millions of people who have lived and died without hearing the gospel on the earth, without the keys of the kingdom. They were not prepared for celestial glory, and there was no power that could prepare them without the keys of this priesthood.

[54]

THE DEGREES OF GLORY

"They must go into prison, both saints and sinners. The good and bad, the righteous and the unrighteous must go to the house of prison, or paradise, and Jesus went and opened the doors of salvation to them. And unless they lost the keys of salvation on account of transgression, as has been the case on this earth, spirits clothed with the priesthood have ministered to them from that day to this. And if they lost the keys by transgression, some one who had been in the flesh, Joseph, for instance, had to take those keys to them. And he is calling one after another to his aid, as the Lord sees he wants help. * * * He is there attending to the business of his mission, and if they did lose the keys of the Priesthood in the spirit world, as they have formerly done on the earth, Joseph has restored those keys to the spirits in prison, so that we who now live on the earth, in the day of salvation and redemption for the house of Israel and the house of Esau, may go forth and officiate for all who died without the gospel and the knowledge of God.

"All that have lived or will live on this earth, will have the privilege of receiving the gospel. They will have apostles, prophets and ministers there, as we have here, to guide them in the ways of truth and righteousness, and lead them back to God. All will have a chance for salvation and eternal life. What do you think of that gospel? No one will be denied the privilege of having it. Where is there a sectarian that can tell you anything about the power of the gospel?

"When you lay down this tabernacle, where are you going? Into the spirit world. Are you going into Abraham's bosom? No, not anywhere nigh there, but into the spirit world. Where is the spirit world? It is right here. Do the good and evil spirits go together? Yes, they do. Do they both inhabit one kingdom? Yes, they do. Do they go to the sun? No. Do they go beyond the boundaries of this organized earth? No, they do not. They are brought forth upon this earth, for the express purpose of inhabiting it to all eternity. Where else are you going? Nowhere else, only as you may be permitted.

"The spirit of Joseph, I do not know that it is just now

in this bowery, but I will assure you it is close to the Latter-day Saints, is active in preaching to the spirits in prison, and preparing the way to redeem the nations of the earth, those who lived in darkness previous to the introduction of the Gospel by himself in these days. He has just as much labor on hand as I have; he has just as much to do. Father Smith and Carlos and Brother Partridge, yes, and every other good saint, are just as busy in the spirit world as you and I are here. They can see us, but we cannot see them, unless our eyes were opened. What are they doing there? They are preaching, preaching all the time and preparing the way for us to hasten our work in building temples here and elsewhere. * * * They are hurrying to get ready by the time that we are ready, and we are all hurrying to get ready by the time our Elder Brother is ready.

"When the faithful Elders, holding this priesthood, go into the spirit world, they carry with them the same power and priesthood that they had while in the mortal tabernacle. They have not the victory over the power of the enemy here, consequently when they leave this world they have perfect control over those evil spirits, and they can not be buffeted by Satan. But as long as they live in the flesh no being on this earth of the posterity of Adam, can be free from the power of the devil.

"Spirits are just as familiar with spirits as bodies are with bodies, though spirits are composed of matter so refined as not to be tangible to this coarser organization. They walk, converse, and have their meetings; and the spirits of good men like Joseph, and the Elders, who have left this Church on earth for a season to operate in another sphere, are rallying all their powers, and going from place to place preaching the Gospel, and Joseph is directing them, saying, go ahead, my brethren, and if they hedge up your way, walk up and command them to disperse. You have the priesthood and can disperse them, but if any of them wish to hear the Gospel, preach to them. Can they baptize them? No. What can they do? They can preach the Gospel, and when we have the privilege of building up Zion, the time will come for saviors to come up on Mount Zion. Some of those who are not in mortality will come along and say, 'Here are a thousand names I wish you to attend to in this temple, and when you have got through with them I will give you another thousand;' and the Elders of Israel and their wives will go forth to officiate for their forefathers, the men for the men and the women for the women."

From "The Contributor," Vol. X, No. 9, July, 1889.

ॐ

HIGHER ORDINANCES TO OPERATE IN NEXT WORLD

By PRESIDENT BRIGHAM YOUNG

"Now a few words to the brethren and sisters upon the doctrine and ordinances of the house of God. All who have lived on the earth according to the best light they had, and would have received the fulness of the Gospel had it been preached to them, are worthy of a glorious resurrection, and will attain to this by being administered for in the flesh by those who have the authority. All others will have a resurrection, and receive a glory, except those who have sinned against the Holy Ghost.

"It is supposed by this people that we have all the ordinances in our possession for life and salvation, and exaltation, and that we are administering in these ordinances. This is not the case. We are in possession of all the ordinances that can be administered in the flesh; but there are other ordinances and administrations that must be administered beyond this world. I know you would ask what they are. I will mention one. We have not, neither can we receive here, the ordinance and the keys of the resurrection. They will be given to those who have passed off this stage of action and have received their bodies again, as many have already done and many more will. They will be ordained, by those who hold the keys of the resurrection, to go forth and resurrect the Saints, just as we receive the ordinance of baptism, then the keys of authority to baptize others for the remission of their sins. This is one of the ordinances we can not receive here, and there are many more. We hold the authority to dispose of, alter and change the elements; but we have not received authority to organize native element to even make a spear of grass grow. We have no such ordinance here. We organize according to men in the flesh. By combining the elements and planting the seed, we cause vegetables, trees, grains, etc., to come forth. We are organizing a kingdom here according to the pattern that the Lord has given for people in the flesh, but not for those who have received the resurrection, although it is a similitude. Another item: We have not the power in the flesh to create and bring forth or produce a spirit; but we have the power to produce a temporal body. The germ of this, God has placed within us. And when our spirits receive our bodies, and through our faithfulness we are worthy to be crowned, we will then receive authority to produce both spirit and body. But these keys we cannot receive in the flesh. Herein, brethren, you can perceive that we have not finished, and cannot finish our work, while we live here, no more than Jesus did while he was in the flesh.

"We cannot receive, while in the flesh, the keys to form and fashion kingdoms and to organize matter, for they are beyond our capacity and calling, beyond this world. In the resurrection, men who have been faithful and diligent in all things in the flesh, have kept their first and second estate and are worthy to be crowned Gods, even the sons of God, will be ordained to organize matter. How much matter do you suppose there is between here and some of the fixed stars which we can see? Enough to frame many, very many millions of such earths as this, yet it is now so diffused, clear and pure, that we look through it and behold the stars. Yet the matter is there. Can you form any conception of this? Can you form any idea of the minuteness of matter? * * *

I am going to stop my talking by saying that, in the millennium, when the kingdom of God is established on the earth in power, glory and perfection, and the reign of wickedness that has so long prevailed is subdued, the Saints of God will have the privilege of building their temples, and of entering into them, becoming, as it were, pillars in the temples of God, and they will officiate for their dead. Then we will see our friends come up, and perhaps some that we have been acquainted with here. If we ask who will stand at the head of the resurrection in this last dispensation, the answer is—Joseph Smith, Junior, the Prophet of God. He is the man who will be resurrected and receive the keys of the resurrection, and he will seal this authority upon others, and they will hunt up their friends and resurrect them when they shall have been officiated for, and bring them up. And we will have revelations to know our forefathers clear back to Father Adam and Mother Eve, and we will enter into the temples of God and officiate for them. Then man will be sealed to man until the chain is made perfect back to Adam, so that there will be a perfect chain of priesthood from Adam to the winding-up scene."

Journal of Discourses, Vol. 9, p. 315.

JOSEPH SMITH HOLDS THE KEYS OF THE LAST DISPENSATION

By PRESIDENT BRIGHAM YOUNG

"Joseph Smith holds the keys of this last dispensation, and is now engaged behind the veil in the great work of the last days. I can tell our beloved brother Christians who have slain the Prophets and butchered and otherwise caused the death of thousands of Latter-day Saints, the priests who have thanked God in their prayers and thanksgiving from the pulpit that we have been plundered, driven, and slain, and the deacons under the pulpit, and their brethren and sisters in their closets, who have thanked God, thinking that the Latter-day Saints were wasted away, something that no doubt will mortify them—something that, to say the least, is a matter of deep regret to them—namely, that no man or woman in this dispensation will ever enter into the Celestial Kingdom of God without the

[59]

consent of Joseph Smith. From the day that the Priesthood was taken from the earth to the winding-up scene of all things, every man and woman must have the certificate of Joseph Smith, junior, as a passport to their entrance into the mansion where God and Christ are—I with you and you with me. I cannot go there without his consent. He holds the keys of that kingdom for the last dispensation—the keys to rule in the spirit world; and he rules there triumphantly, for he gained full power and a glorious victory over the power of Satan while he was yet in the flesh, and was a martyr to his religion and to the name of Christ, which gives him a most perfect victory in the spirit world. He reigns there as supreme a being in his sphere, capacity, and calling, as God does in heaven. Many will exclaim, 'Oh, that is very disagreeable! It is preposterous! We cannot bear the thought!' But it is true.

"I will now tell you something that ought to comfort every man and woman on the face of the earth. Joseph Smith, junior, will again be on this earth, dictating plans and calling for his brethren to be baptized for the very characters who wish this was not so, in order to bring them into a kingdom to enjoy, perhaps, the presence of angels or the spirits of good men, if they cannot endure the presence of the Father and the Son; and he will never cease his operations, under the directions of the Son of God, until the last ones of the children of men are saved that can be, from Adam till now.

"Should not this thought comfort all people? They will, by and by, be a thousand times more thankful for such a man as Joseph Smith, junior, than it is possible for them to be for any earthly good whatever. It is his mission to see that all the children of men in this last dispensation are saved, that can be, through the redemption. You will be thankful, every one of you, that Joseph Smith, junior, was ordained to this great calling before the worlds were. I told you that the doctrine of election and reprobation is a true doctrine. It was decreed in the counsels of eternity, long before the foundations of the earth were laid, that he should be the man, in the last dispensation of this world, to bring forth the word of God to the people, and receive the fulness of the keys and power of the Priesthood of the Son of God. The Lord had his eye upon him, and upon his father, and upon his father's father, and upon their progenitors clear back to Abraham, and from Abraham to the flood, from the flood to Enoch, and from Enoch to Adam. He has watched that family and that blood as it has circulated from its fountain to the birth of that man. He was foreordained in eternity to preside over this last dispensation."

Journal of Discourses, Vol. VII, p. 289-290.

৪৯

WILL ALL BE DAMNED, EXCEPT LATTER-DAY SAINTS?

By PRESIDENT BRIGHAM YOUNG

"It may be asked whether any person can be saved, except those who are baptized. Yes, all the inhabitants of the earth will be saved, except those that sin against the Holy Ghost. Will they come into the presence of the Father and the Son? Not unless they are baptized for the remission of sins, and live faithfully in the observance of the words of life, all the rest of their days. 'In my Father's house are many mansions.' 'Enter ye in at the strait gate; for wide is the gate, and broad is the way that leadeth to destruction, and many there be which go in thereat; because straight is the gate and narrow is the way, which leadeth unto life, and few there be that find it.' A question was asked Joseph Smith if all would be damned, except the Latter-day Saints. He answered 'yes, and most of the Latter-day Saints, unless they repent and do better than they have done.'*

"The glory of those who are not permitted to enter into the presence of the Father and the Son will be greater than mortals can imagine, in glory, excellencey, exquisite pleasure, and intense bliss. It has not entered into the heart of man to

---

*The exact record of this incident will be found in Vol. 3, p. 28 of the History of the Church, as copied from the Elders Journal, Vol. 1, No. 11: "Will everybody be damned, but Mormons," to which the Prophet replied: "Yes, and a great portion of them, unless they repent, and work righteousness."

conceive of the greatness of their glory. But the glory of those who enter in the presence of God exceeds all these in glory, as the light of the sun exceeds the light of the moon and stars. All these different glories are ordained to fit the capacities and conditions of men."

Journal of Discourses, Vol. 9, *p.* 315.

ૐ

UNIVERSAL SALVATION

By PRESIDENT BRIGHAM YOUNG

"How many Gods there are, and how many places there are in their kingdoms, is not for me to say; but I can say this, which is a source of much comfort, consolation, and gratification to me: Behold the goodness, the long-suffering, the kindness, and the strong parental feeling of our Father and God in preparing the way and providing the means to save the children of men,—not alone the Latter-day Saints—not those alone who have the privilege of the first principles of the celestial law, but to save all. It is a universal salvation—a universal redemption. Do not conclude that I am a Universalist, as the term is generally understood, although that doctrine is true in part, like the doctrines or professions of all professing Christians. As was stated yesterday, by one of those who spoke, when he was a Methodist he enjoyed a portion of the Spirit of the Lord. Hundreds of those now present have had a like experience in a greater or less degree, before they joined this Church. Then, when we inquire who will be saved, I answer, All will be saved, as Jesus said, when speaking to the Apostles, except the sons of perdition. They will be saved through the atonement and their own good works, according to the law that is given to them. Will the heathen be saved? Yes, so far as they have lived according to the best light and intelligence they had; but not in the Celestial Kingdom. Who will not be saved? Those who have received the truth, or had the privilege of receiving it, and then rejected it. They are the only ones who will become the sons of predition, go into everlasting punishment, and become angels to the Devil.

THE DEGREES OF GLORY

"The Priesthood the Lord has again bestowed upon those who will receive it, is for the express purpose of preparing them to become proficient in the principles pertaining to the law of the Celestial Kingdom. If we obey this law, preserve it inviolate, live according to it, we shall be prepared to enjoy the blessings of a Celestial Kingdom. Will any others? Yes, thousands and millions of the inhabitants of the earth who would have received and obeyed the law that we preach, if they had had the privilege. When the Lord shall bring again Zion, and the watchmen shall see eye to eye, and Zion shall be established, saviours will come upon Mount Zion, and save all the sons and daughters of Adam that are capable of being saved, by administering for them. Is not this pleasing? Is it not gratifying? Is it not a consoling feeling and influence upon the mind of every intelligent being? Our former views were that the majority of the inhabitants of the earth would not be saved in any kind of a kingdom of glory, but would inherit a kingdom of damnation. Jesus said, 'In my Father's house are many mansions. If it were not so, I would have told you. I go to prepare a place for you, that where I am ye may be also.' In other words, 'I go to prepare a place for you who have received and obeyed the celestial law, which I have committed to you.' The celestial is the highest of all. The telestial and terrestrial are also spoken of; and how many more kingdoms of glory there are is not for me to say. I do not know that they are not innumerable. This is a source of great joy to me.

"One of the brethren, yesterday, felt so rejoiced, under like reflections, that he said he could pray for the devils in hell, if it would do any good. It is not for us to pray for them, because they have become sons of perdition. You may pray for your persecutors—for those who hate you, and revile you, and speak all manner of evil of you, if they do it ignorantly; but if they do it understandingly, justice must take its course in regard to them; and except they repent, they will become sons of perdition. This is my testimony. * * *

"There is a chance for those who have lived and for those who now live. The Gospel has come. Truth and light and righteousness are sent forth into the world, and those who

[63]

receive them will be saved in the Celestial Kingdom of God. And many of those who, through ignorance, through tradition, superstition, and the erroneous precepts of the fathers, do not receive them, and yet inherit a good and glorious kingdom, and will enjoy more and receive more than ever entered into the heart of man to conceive, unless he has had a revelation.

"My heart is comforted. I behold the people of God, that they have been hunted, cast out, driven from the face of men. The powers of earth and hell have striven to destroy this kingdom from the earth. The wicked have succeeded in doing so in former ages; but this kingdom they cannot destroy, because it is the last dispensation—because it is the fulness of times. It is the dispensation of all dispensations, and will excel in magnificence and glory every dispensation that has ever been committed to the children of men upon this earth. The Lord will bring again Zion, redeem his Israel, plant his standard upon the earth, and establish the laws of his kingdom, and those laws will prevail. No law can issue from man or from any body of men to govern and control in eternal things; consequently, those laws must come from heaven to govern and control both Saint and sinner, believer and un-believer, and every character upon the earth; and they will be issued according to the capacity, knowledge, and mode of life of the people to whom they are promulgated."

Journal of Discourses, Vol. 8, pp. 35-36.

ॐ

THE NEGROES YET TO POSSESS THE PRIESTHOOD

By President Brigham Young

"I have endeavored to give you a few items relating to the Celestial Kingdom of God and to the other kingdoms which the Lord has prepared for his children. The Lamanites or Indians are just as much the children of our Father and God as we are. So also are the Africans. But we are also the children of adoption through obedience to the Gospel of his

Son. Why are so many of the inhabitants of the earth cursed with a skin of blackness? It comes in consequence of their fathers rejecting the power of the Holy Priesthood and the law of God. They will go down to death. And when all the rest of the children have received their blessings in the Holy Priesthood, then that curse will be removed from the seed of Cain, and they will then come up and possess the Priesthood, and receive all the blessings which we now are entitled to.

"The volition of the creature is free; this is a law of their existence, and the Lord cannot violate his own law; were He to do that, he would cease to be God. He has placed life and death before his children, and it is for them to choose. If they choose life, they receive the blessings of life; if they choose death, they must abide the penalty. This is a law which has always existed from all eternity, and will continue to exist throughout all the eternities to come. Every intelligent being must have the power of choice, and God brings forth the results of the acts of His creatures to promote His kingdom and subserve His purposes in the salvation and exaltation of His children. If the Lord could have His own way, He would have all the human family to enter into His church and kingdom, receive the Holy Priesthood, and come into the Celestial Kingdom of our Father and God, by the power of their own choice."

Journal of Discourses, Vol. 11, p. 272.

"We have this illustrated in the account of Cain and Abel. Cain conversed with his God every day and knew all about the plan of creating this earth for his Father told him. But for the want of humility and, through jealousy and an anxiety to possess the kingdom and to have the whole of it under his own control and not allow anybody else the right to say one word, what did he do? He killed his brother. The Lord put a mark on him and there are some of his children in this room. When all the other children of Adam have had the privilege of receiving the priesthood and of coming into the kingdom of God and of being redeemed from the four quarters of the earth, and have received their resurrection from the dead, then it will be time enough to remove the curse from Cain and his posterity. He deprived his brother of the privilege of pursuing his journey through life, and of extending his kingdom by multiplying on the earth and because he did this, he is the last to share the joys of the kingdom of God."

Journal of Discourses, Vol. 2, pp. 142-3.

ह❦

TEMPLE BUILDING AND THE MEANING OF THE ENDOWMENT

By PRESIDENT BRIGHAM YOUNG
(Sermon delivered in the Tabernacle, April 6, 1853.)

"Soon after, the Church, through our beloved Prophet Joseph, was commanded to build a Temple to the Most High in Kirtland, Ohio, and this was the next House of the Lord we hear of on the earth, since the days of Solomon's Temple. Joseph not only received revelation and commandment to build a Temple, but received a pattern also, as did Moses for the Tabernacle, and Solomon for his Temple; for without a pattern, he could not know what was wanting, having never seen one, and not having experienced its use.

"Without revelation Joseph could not know what was wanting, any more than any other man, and, without commandment, the Church were too few in numbers, too weak in faith, and too poor in purse, to attempt such a mighty enterprise. But by means of all these stimulants, a mere handful of men, living on air, and a little hominy and milk, and often salt or no salt when milk could not be had; the great Prophet Joseph, in the stone quarry, quarrying rock with his own hands; and the few men in the Church, following his example of obedience and diligence wherever most needed; with laborers on the walls, holding the sword in one hand to protect themselves from the mob, while they placed the stone and moved the trowel with the other, the Kirtland Temple, the second House of the Lord that we have any published record of on the earth, was so far completed as to be dedicated. And those

[66]

first Elders who helped to build it, received a portion of their first endowments, or we might say more clearly, some of the first, or introductory, or initiatory ordinances, preparatory to an endowment.

"The preparatory ordinances there administered, though accompanied by the ministration of angels, and the presence of the Lord Jesus, were but a faint similitude of the ordinances of the House of the Lord in their fulness; yet many, through the instigation of the devil, thought they had received all, and knew as much as God; they have apostatized, and gone to hell. But be assured, brethren, there are but few, very few of the Elders of Israel, now on earth, who know the meaning of the word endowment. To know, they must experience; and to experience, a Temple must be built.

"Let me give you the definition in brief. Your endowment is to receive all those ordinances in the House of the Lord, which are necessary for you, after you have departed this life, to enable you to walk back to the presence of the Father, passing the angels who stand as sentinels, being enabled to give them the key words, the signs and tokens, pertaining to the Holy Priesthood, and gain your eternal exaltation in spite of earth and hell.

"Who has received and understands such an endowment in this assembly? You need not answer. Your voices would be few and far between, yet the keys to these endowments are among you, and thousands have received them, so that the devil, with all his aids, need not suppose he can again destroy the Holy Priesthood from the earth, by killing a few, for he cannot do it. God has set His hand, for the last time, to redeem His people, the honest in heart, and Lucifer cannot hinder Him.

"Before these endowments could be given at Kirtland, the Saints had to flee before mobocracy. And, by toil and daily labor, they found places in Missouri, where they laid the corner stones of Temples, in Zion and her Stakes, and then had to retreat to Illinois, to save the lives of those who could get away alive from Missouri, where fell the Apostle David W. Patten, with many like associates, and where they were imprisoned in

THE VISION

loathsome dungeons, and fed on human flesh,* Joseph and Hyrum, and many others. But before all this had transpired, the Temple at Kirtland had fallen into the hands of wicked men, and by them been polluted, like the Temple of Jerusalem, and consequently it was disowned by the Father and the Son. * * *

"But what of the Temple in Nauvoo. By the aid of sword in one hand, and trowel and hammer in the other, with fire arms at hand, and a strong band of police, and the blessings of heaven, the Saints, through hunger, and thirst, and weariness, and watchings, and prayings, so far completed the Temple, despite the devices of the mob, that many received a small portion of their endowment, but we know of no one who received it in its fullness. And then, to save the lives of all the Saints from cruel murder, we moved westward, and being led by the all-searching eye of the Great Jehovah, we arrived at this place.

"Of our journey hither, we need say nothing only, God led us. Of the sufferings of those who were compelled to, and did, leave Nauvoo in the winter of 1846, we need say nothing. Those who experienced it know it, and those who did not, to tell them of it would be like exhibiting a beautiful painting to a blind man."

Journal of Discourses, Vol. 2, pp. 31-32.

---

*Note: In a letter written from Carthage Jail, Carthage, Illinois, by Joseph A. McRae, dated March 7, 1939, to the compiler of this book, Brother McRae says:

"Respecting the incident you mention: My paternal grandmother told me many times, for I asked her to repeat to me the experiences she had in the early period of the church, and this is what she said, speaking to me: 'I visited my husband several times while he was in the Liberty Jail. I carried letters to and from the Prophet, that were sent by his family. Your father was born at Far West while your grandfather was in prison and I took him to the jail to have him blessed. The Prophet blessed him and gave him the name of Joseph.

" 'Several times when I visited, I sat at the table and ate with them. The food was brought in and we all sat down together. The Prophet always deferred to his brother Hyrum, and as he was the eldest he had Hyrum sit at the head of the table and serve. Any meat that was to be carved was carved by Hyrum. One day a piece of roast meat was brought in that looked very dark, as though it had been burned. Brother Hyrum took the carving knife and fork, put the fork into the meat and they fell from his hands. He picked up the tools again and attempted to carve the meat and they fell from his hands again. After the second attempt, the Prophet said: "Do not touch it, for it is human flesh." It was afterwards told that the guards boasted they had cut a piece of the flesh from the thigh of an old negro and had fed it to the Mormons."

PARENTAL LOVE AND PHYSICAL PERFECTION WILL EXIST IN THE CELESTIAL RESURRECTION

By PRESIDENT BRIGHAM YOUNG

"I think it has been taught by some that as we lay our bodies down, they will so rise again in the resurrection with all the impediments and imperfections that they had here; and that if a wife does not love her husband in this state she cannot love him in the next. This is not so. Those who attain to the blessing of the first or celestial resurrection will be pure and holy and perfect in body. Every man and woman that reaches to this unspeakable attainment will be as beautiful as the angels that surround the throne of God. If you can, by faithfulness in this life, obtain the right to come up in the morning of the resurrection, you need entertain no fears that the wife will be dissatisfied with her husband or the husband with the wife; for those of the first resurrection will be free from sin and from the consequences and power of sin."

Journal of Discourses, Vol. 10, *p.* 24.

THE SALT LAKE TEMPLE SEEN IN VISION IN JULY, 1847

By PRESIDENT BRIGHAM YOUNG

"Though the enemy had power to kill our Prophet, that is, kill his body, did he not accomplish all that was in his heart to accomplish in his day? He did, to my certain knowledge, and I have many witnesses here that heard him declare that he had done everything he could do—he had revealed everything that could be revealed *at present,* he had prepared the way for the people to walk in, and no man or woman should be deprived of going into the presence of the Father and the Son, and enjoying an eternal exaltation, *if they would walk in the path he had pointed out. * * ***

"Some will inquire, 'Do you suppose we shall finish this Temple, brother Brigham?' I have had such questions put to

[69]

me already. My answer is, I do not know, and I do not care any more about it than I should if my body was dead and in the grave, and my spirit in Paradise. I never have cared but for one thing, and that is, simply to know that I am now right before my Father in Heaven. If I am this moment, this day, doing the things God requires of my hands, and precisely where my Father in Heaven wants me to be, I care no more about tomorrow than though it never would come. I do not know where I shall be tomorrow, nor when this Temple will be done—I know no more about it than you do. If God reveals anything for you, I will tell you of it as freely as to say, go to City Creek, and drink until you are satisfied.

"This I do know—there should be a Temple built here. I do know it is the duty of this people to commence to build a Temple. Now, some will want to know what kind of a building it will be. Wait patiently, brethren, until it is done, and put forth your hands willingly to finish it. I know what it will be. I am not a visionary man, neither am I given much to phophesying. When I want any of that done I call on brother Heber—he is my Prophet, he loves to prophesy, and I love to hear him. *I scarcely ever say much about revelations, or visions, but suffice it to say, five years ago last July I was here, and saw in the spirit the Temple not ten feet from where we have laid the chief corner stone. I have not inquired what kind of a Temple we should build. Why? Because it was represented before me. I have never looked upon that ground, but the vision of it was there. I see it as plainly as if it was in reality before me. Wait until it is done. I will say, however, that it will have six towers, to begin with, instead of one.* Now do not any of you apostatize because it will have six towers, and Joseph only built one. It is easier for us to build sixteen than it was for him to build one. *The time will come when there will be one in the centre of Temples we shall build, and on the top, groves and fish ponds. But we shall not see them here, at present.*"

Journal of Discourses, Vol. 1, p. 132-133.

THE DEGREES OF GLORY

DATA ON TEMPLES ERECTED TO DATE (1939) IN THIS DISPENSATION

Name of Temple	Date Dedicated	By Whom Dedicated	Where Recorded
Kirtland	March 27, 1836	Joseph the Prophet	Doc. & Cov., Sec. 109
Nauvoo	May 1, 1846	Elder Orson Hyde	Contributor, Vol. 10:147
			Comp. H. Ch., Vol. 3, p. 22
St. George	April 6, 1877	Elder Daniel H. Wells	Jrnl. His., Apr. 6, 1877
Logan	May 17, 1884	Pres. John Taylor	Mil. Star, Vol. 46:385
Manti	May 21, 1888	Elder Lorenzo Snow	Mil. Star, Vol. 50:886
Salt Lake	April 6, 1893	Pres. Wilford Woodruff	Contributor, 14:292
Hawaiian	Nov. 27, 1919	Pres. Heber J. Grant	Improvement Era, 23:282
Canadian	Aug. 26, 1923	Pres. Heber J. Grant	Improvement Era, 26:1075
Arizona	Oct. 23, 1927	Pres. Heber J. Grant	Improvement Era, 31:96

ॐ

"I HAVE BEEN IN THE SPIRIT WORLD TWO NIGHTS IN SUCCESSION"

Remarks at the Funeral of Jedediah M. Grant on December 4, 1856, in the Tabernacle, Salt Lake City

By HEBER C. KIMBALL

"I went to see him one day last week, and he reached out his hand and shook hands with me; he could not speak, but he shook hands warmly with me. * * * I laid my hands upon him and blessed him, and asked God to strengthen his lungs that he might be easier, and in two or three minutes he raised himself up and talked for about an hour as busily as he could, telling me what he had seen and what he understood, until I was afraid he would weary himself, when I arose and left him.

"He said to me, 'Brother Heber, I have been into the spirit world two nights in succession, and, of all the dreads that ever came across me, the worst was to have to again return to my body, though I had to do it. But O,' says he, 'the order and government that were there! When in the spirit world, I saw the order of righteous men and women; beheld them organized in their several grades, and there appeared to be no obstruction to my vision; I could see every man and women in their grade and order. I looked to see whether there was any disorder there, but there was none; neither could I see any

[71]

death nor any darkness, disorder or confusion.' He said that the people he there saw were organized in family capacities; and when he looked at them he saw grade after grade and all were organized and in perfect harmony. He would mention one item after another and say, 'Why, it is just as brother Brigham says it is; it is just as he told us many a time.'

"That is a testimony as to the truth of what brother Brigham teaches us, and I know it is true, from what little light I have.

"He saw the righteous gathered together in the spirit world, and there were no wicked spirits among them. He saw his wife; she was the first person that came to him. He saw many that he knew, but did not have conversation with any except his wife, Caroline. She came to him, and he said that she looked beautiful and had their little child, that died on the Plains, in her arms, and said, 'Mr. Grant, here is little Margaret; you know that the wolves ate her up, but it did not hurt her; here she is all right.'

" 'To my astonishment,' he said, 'when I looked at families there was a deficiency in some, there was a lack, for I saw families that would not be permitted to come and dwell together, because they had not honored their calling here.'

"He asked his wife, Caroline, where Joseph and Hyrum and Father Smith and others were, she replied, 'they have gone away ahead, to perform and transact business for us.' The same as when brother Brigham and his brethren left Winter Quarters and came here to search out a home; they came to find a location for their brethren.

"He also spoke of the buildings he saw there, remarking that the Lord gave Solomon wisdom and poured gold and silver into his hands that he might display his skill and ability, and said that the temple erected by Solomon was much inferior to the most ordinary buildings he saw in the spirit world.

"In regard to gardens, says brother Grant, 'I have seen good gardens on this earth, but I never saw any to compare with those that were there. I saw flowers of numerous kinds, and some with from fifty to a hundred different colored flowers growing upon one stalk.' We have many kinds of flowers on the earth, and I suppose those very articles came from heaven, or they would not be here.

"After mentioning the things that he had seen, he spoke of how much he disliked to return and resume his body, after having seen the beauty and glory of the spirit world, where the righteous spirits are gathered together.

"Some may marvel at my speaking about these things, for many profess to believe that we have no spiritual existence. But do you not believe that my spirit was organized before it came to my body here? And do you not think there can be houses and gardens, fruit trees, and every other good thing there? The spirits of those things were made, as well as our spirits, and it follows that they can exist upon the same principle.

"After speaking of the gardens and the beauty of every thing there, brother Grant said that he felt extremely sorrowful at having to leave so beautiful a place and come back to earth, for he looked upon his body with loathing, but was obliged to enter it again.

"He said that after he came back he could look upon his family and see the spirit that was in them; and the darkness that was in them; and that he conversed with them about the Gospel, and what they should do, and they replied, 'Well, brother Grant, perhaps it is so, and perhaps it is not,' and said that was the state of this people, to a great extent, for many are full of darkness and will not believe me.

"I never had a view of the righteous assembling in the spirit world, but I have had a view of the hosts of hell, and have seen them as plainly as I see you today. The righteous spirits gather together to prepare and qualify themselves for a future day, and evil spirits have no power over them, though they are constantly striving for the mastery. I have seen evil spirits attempt to overcome those holding the Priesthood, and I know how they act."*

Journal of Discourses, Vol. 4, pp. 135-6-7.

---

*The following references are given among many on the subject of communication of the living with the departed, which will be of great interest to those who desire additional light on the subject:

THE VISION

THE REDEMPTION OF THE DEAD

By Orson Pratt

"Many will inquire, what will be the condition of those who have died before this light was revealed? We answer that God has made provisions in the laws, ordinances, and plans, instituted before the foundation of the world, to suit the circumstances of every individual. Those who die without hearing a message sent by authority from Heaven, do not reject it; and God has ordained that, in the dispensation of the fulness of times, the living shall officiate for the dead. For this cause God has commanded a Temple to be built, that those ordinances necessary for the salvation and redemption of the dead may be revealed and administered in the same. The word of the Lord which came unto Joseph the Seer, shows the importance of these things; it read as follows:

" 'Verily I say unto you, that your anointings, and your washings, and your baptisms for the dead, and your solemn assemblies, and your memorials for your sacrifices, by the sons of Levi, and for your oracles in your most holy places, wherein you receive conversations, and your statutes and judgments, for the beginning of the revelations and foundation of Zion, and for the glory, honor, and endowment of all her municipals, are ordained by the ordinance of my holy house, which my people are always commanded to build unto my holy name.'

"We understand, by this revelation, that God's people are always commanded to build unto His holy name a house, wherein baptisms, and all other necessary ordinances may be legally administered, not only for the living, but also for, and in the name of, and in behalf of, the dead. If the spirits of the

---

A series of articles, entitled: "The Undiscovered Country," by Elder Orson F. Whitney, Improvement Era, Vol. 23.

Two articles, entitled: "The Veil: Its Use and Abuse," by Prof. N. L. Nelson, Improvement Era, Vol. 32.

Two articles, entitled: "Raised from the Dead," by LeRoi C. Snow, Improvement Era, Vol. 32.

Parley P. Pratt comforted by his deceased wife, Autobiography of Parley P. Pratt, 1888 Ed., p. 261.

Heber C. Kimball dictates lost history to his son Solomon, Improvement Era, Vol. 11, p. 583.

dead who are in prison will hearken unto the messages of those holding the Priesthood, who are sent to their prison-houses to open the prison doors, and set them free; if they will believe in Jesus Christ, and repent of all their sins, and receive the glad tidings of redemption; if they will receive by faith what their friends in the flesh have done for them through the ordinances of God's holy house, namely, the baptisms, confirmations, ordinations, washings, anointings, signs, tokens, keys, and sealing powers which are administered by the living, and unto the living, for, and in the name of, the dead; if they will, with sincerity of faith and humble repentance, believe in and receive all that is done in their behalf, as the living receive what Christ has done, they shall be redeemed from their prisons, and their names shall be recorded among the sanctified in the Celestial Kingdom, and the records in heaven will be according to the records of God's holy house upon the earth; and that which is done and sealed on the earth, for and in their behalf, will be acknowledged, recorded, and sealed in the heavens, and will be valid and legal in the great day of the resurrection of the righteous; but the remainder of the spirits who will not receive the glad tidings, and accept of deliverance, shall be kept in chains of darkness, unto the judgment of the great day, and their torment shall be as if suffering in flames of fire, where their worm dieth not.

"Do you inquire how we are to obtain the genealogies of our fathers, so as to do this work for them which they, when living, had not the opportunity of doing, and which they, as spirits in prison, cannot do? We answer, that it is the duty of all Saints among all nations to search out, as far as possible, your family records, and your genealogies, and your kindred, both the living and the dead. And when you have been diligent, and have procured all the information within your reach, and have gone into the holy Temple of the Most High, and done what is required of the living for the dead, then God will show you, by his Prophets and Seers, and by holy messengers and angels, the genealogies of your fathers, back from generation to generation, unto the beginning, or unto the time when the powers, and keys, and ordinances of the Priesthood were upon the earth. When you obtain these genealogies, it will be your duty to receive in the holy Temple, all the ordinances and sealing powers which were instituted in the councils of the Sons of God before the world was, for the salvation, redemption, exaltation, glory, and honor of the dead who died without a knowledge of these things; for you, without your fathers, cannot be made perfect, neither can the ancient fathers who held the Priesthood be made perfect without the children.

"The time is near at hand when the fathers who hold the Priesthood in Heaven, will be united with the children who hold the Priesthood upon the earth; but there are many generations intervening, who held not the Priesthood, but died in their ignorance; the grand chain of Patriarchal government, according to the order of generations, will be broken, and the union will not be complete, unless the hearts of the fathers are turned to seek after the redemption of the generations of their children who have laid down in their graves in the days of darkness; and also unless the hearts of the children are turned towards their fathers. Thus through the united exertions of the Priesthood in Heaven, with the Priesthood upon the earth, the intermediate links of the great chain of generation will be restored, and the union of the fathers with the children will be made perfect, and each successive generation will stand in their own order, exercising their Patriarchal authority and swaying the sceptre of righteousness, according to the holy order of the Priesthood forever and ever.

"When these holy and sacred institutions are made known to the spirits in prison by holy messengers holding the Priesthood, they will be left to their own agency, either to receive or reject these glad tidings, and will be judged according to men in the flesh who have the privilege of hearing the same things. By the same law they shall be justified, and by the same law they shall be condemned, according to their works; thus God has ordained the same plan for the salvation of both the living and the dead; for those that die in ignorance, as for those who hear it while in the flesh."

"The Seer," pp. 141-142.

THE INCREASED POWERS AND CAPACITIES OF MAN IN HIS FUTURE STATE

By ORSON PRATT

"* * * Now, shall we be made like the Lord, or are we some other species of beings, so far disconnected with Him that we never need expect to reach this high standard? How is it? Who are we? We are told by divine revelation that we are the Sons of God; we are told in the vision received by the Prophet Joseph, concerning these different creations, that 'the inhabitants thereof are begotten sons and daughters unto God.' Indeed! Begotten sons and daughters unto God? The inhabitants of these creations? Yes. This agrees with what the New and Old Testaments, and the various revelations which God has given, clearly declare—that God is the Father of our Spirits. A writer in the New Testament says, 'Beloved, now are we the sons of God,' that is, in this life—'but it does not yet appear what we shall be, but when he shall appear we shall be like him.' Not unlike him, not so far separated from him that the one will be finite and other infinite; but 'we shall be like Him.'

"This is consistent and reasonable. Every species of being with which we are acquainted begets its own kind, and the young thereof, whether man, quadrupeds, fowls or fish, finally grow up and become like their parents. This is a universal law of nature, so far as we know; therefore, if we are begotten sons and daughters of God, if we are His offspring, He is our Father, and why separate man from all the rest of creation, and say that he can never become like his Father? If all other beings become like their parents, why not we attain to the same? And if our Father and God can pierce all those creations mentioned by Enoch, and His eye discerns what is going on in the midst of them all, why may not His children become like Him in this respect? This is what the beloved disciple, John the Revelator, one of the Apostles of Christ, meant. He says, 'Now are we the Sons of God, and it doth not yet appear what we shall be; but when He shall appear, we shall be like Him.' He knew that much, though he did not comprehend all of the perfect capacities of man in this state. Though we are chained down here by the laws of nature, yet realizing that we are the children of that Almighty being who controls universal nature, and all the worlds that are spoken of, we expect to come up, and that the attributes which our eternal Father possesses will be fully developed in us, and that we also shall be able to penetrate the immensity of space and gaze upon the workmanship of our Father's hands.

"It is concerning us that we shall be in the presence of God when we become immortal and perfect beings. We are now not in his presence; the fall has let down a veil between us and our Father and God. This veil does not prevent the eye of the Almighty from seeing and discerning the conduct of his children, but it prevents us, while in this state of mortality, from beholding his presence, unless we rend the veil by our faith and obedience and, like the brother of Jared, are permitted to come back into his presence. But to be in the presence of God is it absolutely necessary that our earth should be wafted away from its present orbit in the solar system and carried off to some immense distance in space? Is this really necessary? What are we to understand by being in the presence of God? Is it necessary, to do so, that we should be in the same vicinity or within a few yards or feet of him? I think not. We are now laboring under the imperfections of the fall, and because of that fall a veil shuts us from his presence; but let the effects of the fall be removed and mankind be able to again look upon the face of their Father and Creator, and they will be in his presence.

"Will the spirits of men, before they receive their resurrected body, return into the presence of God? Yes. Read what Alma said to his son Corianton on this subject, describing the state of the spirit between the time of death and the resurrection. He says, 'It has been made known to me by an angel that the spirits of all men, as soon as they are dead, whether wicked or righteous, shall return home to that God who gave them life;' that is, they go back into His presence. The wicked, however, are again cast out into outer darkness, the

[78]

light of the countenance of their Lord is again withdrawn
from them, a veil is let down between them and their Father
and God. But how is it with the righteous? When they go
back and behold the face of their Father they will continue
in the light of His countenance, and have the privilege of seeing Him. They have returned to their ancient home, to that
God who gave them life, to the mansions and familiar places
where they dwelt ages and ages before they came here. They
have gone back to meet with familiar acquaintances, and their
memories will be so increased and perfected after they leave
this body that the things of their former state and condition
will be fresh to them, and they will look upon this little speck
called time, in which they have dwelt seventy, eighty or ninety
years, as but a dream or night vision during which the things
of former ages were shut from their memories; but when they
get back to their ancient home they will have a bright recollection of all these things, and of the familiar countenance of their
Father, and the countenance of His only begotten Son, and the
countenances of the millions on millions of their brother and
sister spirits, with whom they once lived. And the memories
of the wicked, after they leave this body, will be so increased
that they will have a bright recollection, Alma says, of all their
guilt. Here they forget a good many things wherein they
have displeased God; but in that condition, even before the
resurrection, they will have a bright recollection of all their
guilt, which will kindle in them a flame like that of an un-
quenchable fire, creating in their bosoms a feeling of torment,
pain and misery, because they have sinned against their own
Father and their own God, and rejected His counsels.

"To go back, then, into the presence of God, is to be
placed in a condition wherein His presence can be seen. It
does not mean, in all cases, that people who return into His
presence are immediately placed within a few yards, or rods,
or within a short distance of His person. Is there any revelation to prove this? Yes. I have already quoted what the
Lord said in relation to all these creations. He said that from
the whole of them which he had made he had taken Zion to
His own bosom. Now if He has taken Zion to His own

[79]

bosom from all these numberless creations, can they all be concentrated in a little spot of a few rods in diameter in order to get into His presence? Why no. If each Zion did not occupy any more space than one particle of our globe, yet inasmuch as the worlds are more numberless than the particles of millions of earths like this, how could they all get into so small a space as to get near to the person of the Lord? They could not do it. But suffice it to say the veil is removed, and no matter how distant a redeemed world may be it will be in the presence of God.

"In order to make it familiar let me bring up an illustration well known among the children of mortality. For instance, we have, within the present century, invented methods of communicating by telegraph, by means of which, with the proper facilities, we in this room in Ogden can converse with the people in London and they, by means of the wires laid on the bed of the great Atlantic Ocean, can reply in about two seconds. This wonderful invention has, in some measure, diminished the distance between the inhabitants of Ogden and those of London, has it not? The people of the last century and of centuries preceding would have had to wait for a long period of time before they could get a communication from London; but now a few seconds are all that is necessary. We will suppose that it was within the scope of man's power—which it is not—to hear as well as to converse through the aid of the telegraph line. Supposing that by such means we could hear the people in London or that there was a facility for so doing, such as is mentioned in the Doctrine and Covenants, when the first angel shall sound, by which the people of all the earth will hear the words that he speaks: I say, supposing there was such a principle brought into operation so that we could actually hear the words spoken by the people in London, would not that also diminish the impressions of distance? Now supposing still further, that there was a principle differing from our natural light, a principle of light of a more refined nature, that could penetrate from London to this point, so that it would affect our eyes, enabling us to see persons there, then we could both see and hear them at eight or nine thousand miles distant. Would we not be in their presence? Would it be really necessary for us to travel eight or nine thousand miles, to get into the same room with them, in order to get into their presence? We should consider ourselves in their presence if we could see them; and if in addition to this we could communicate with and make them hear us, we should feel all that familiarity and sociability that we should if we were within a few steps of them. I look upon the condition of things in this respect in a future state as somewhat similar to that. If you or I lived upon one of the most remote stars that has ever been seen by the most powerful telescopic instrument invented by man, from which it would take light, traveling at the immense rate of one hundred and ninety-two thousand miles every beat of the pulse, six hundred thousand years to reach this planetary system; I say, suppose we were living on one of these very remote bodies, and suppose there was a principle pervading all space, that would transmit to the immortal eyes much more swiftly than the natural light, and that 192,000 miles a second would be considered a very slow motion compared with that still more refined light that shines forth from the personage of our Father and God; and supposing that our eyes were so constructed and adapted that we could behold the light of His countenance without traversing this space, or in a time much less than six hundred thousand years, but still taking a certain length of time to go all that distance, would we not be in the presence of God? If every world has got to be removed into his presence one by one, and all the inhabitants thereof, how many millions on millions of ages would it take, before all these successively could enter into His presence so as to be near Him? If each world should roll into His presence successively, and then give place to others, we should be out of His presence almost continually, for all those worlds I have named are not a beginning, not even a beginning to the number of His creations, and yet if they had to come along and be successively rolled into his presence, so as to be near Him personally, if each one stayed there only five minutes, there is no man who could calculate or realize anything about the almost infinite duration that would have to elapse before they could come around a second time into His presence. Hence there is something more perfect in the construction of the works of the Almighty that lets man into His presence whatsoever part of the universe he may exist in—we may have the veil removed, and His presence becomes visible.

"Can they converse with Him when situated at these immense distances from His person? Yes. How? Through those more perfect faculties which God will give to immortal man. It is as easy for His children, when they are perfected and made like him, to converse with Him at these immense distances and for their eyes to pierce all these creations as it is for their Father and God to do so.

"Thus we see that man is a God in embryo, agreeing with that which the Lord has revealed to us in the vision given to Joseph. 'They shall be Gods, even the Sons of God,' growing up like their Father, their bodies fashioned like His glorious body. The attributes and faculties with which man is endowed in a mortal state are godlike in their nature, but they are weakened and incapable of any very great expansion by being shut up in this frail mortal body; but when we are freed from mortality we have the promise that we shall become like him, and if He can grasp in His comprehension and vision all these numberless creations, so will those who are made like Him be able to do the same.

"There are many other things that would be profitable to dwell upon in discussing the increased capacities and powers of man in his future state besides the physical qualities I have spoken of. There is his increased knowledge and the proportionate increase of power that will accompany it; the great creative principle, the mechanical work which was performed by our Father and God in constructing creations, and in redeeming and glorifying them; that great principle of knowledge by which our Father and God can call forth from a shapeless mass of dust an immortal tabernacle, into which enters an immortal spirit. All these principles of wisdom, knowledge and power will be given to his children, and will enable them to organize the elements, form creations, and call forth from the dust intelligent beings, who will be under their charge and control. These things might be spoken of, had we time this evening; indeed it is a subject that is almost inexhaustible in its nature. When we commence to speak upon it we scarcely know where to begin and having launched out upon it, we scarcely know where to end, for there is no end to it.

"Man is destined for all future duration, to act in the capacity of a celestial being. The faculties he now possesses in embryo are but little understood, yet we ocassionally see them developed among holy men, as in the case of Enoch, Moses and Abraham, who had the Urim and Thummim, and who were able to behold many of those creations of which I have spoken. Among the many attributes and powers which man will possess in a future state, I will mention that of being able to comprehend more than one thing at a time. Here we are chained down to one thing at a time, and while a man is attending to and trying to comprehend one thing he almost loses sight of everything else, except it be some few things that are very familiar to him. If he undertakes to work a mathematical problem, he can not, at the same time, work out a hundred problems more, and come to a conclusion in regard to them. He has to concentrate his mind on one subject and bring forth the demonstration step by step in order to arrive at certain conclusions.

"Will man in a future state have increased faculties in regard to this? Yes. Our Heavenly Father notices every hair of the heads of the children of men that falls to the ground; not one of your hairs shall fall to the ground, says Jesus, unnoticed by your Father which is in heaven. If he were noticing a hair falling from my head, could He notice at the same time the falling of a hair from your head? Yes; and if the hair were falling from the heads of every individual on the earth at the same instant, He could notice the whole of it, for He has this increased faculty by which He can grasp in His vision myriads of things to come.

"We might also speak of the faculty of going back into the past ages of eternity, and comprehending works that have been millions of ages in progress, also that faculty of seeing and comprehending that which will take place in the future ages of eternity, for millions of years to come. Here we prophesy in part, and here we have knowledge in part; here we gaze upon one thing at once; here we can comprehend the future in some measure. But we 'see through a glass darkly.' then we shall see face to face; then knowledge in part will be done away, for the past, present and future, and millions on millions of creations will come before us and be alike comprehended by the vision of immortal man."

*(Excerpts from lecture delivered in Ogden, Utah,
on January 27, 1874.)*
Journal of Discourses, Vol. 16, pp. 363-8.

ह‌ॐ

THE EARTH TO BE CELESTIALIZED

By ORSON PRATT

"* * * The earth will be shaped into the form best adapted to the occupation of a higher order of beings. Now, children of mortality occupy this globe. In some portions of the earth we suffer extremes of heat and cold. The Laplander has guarded against this in his snow house, while the people of the torrid regions have to guard against intense heat. And there is much suffering by the inhabitants of the earth, in their present state of mortality, from the extremes of heat and cold. But in relation to the great event I have named, I have no doubt but what every motion and arrangement that the Lord will cause to take place upon the surface of our globe will have a tendency to prepare it for the habitation of beings of a higher order of intelligence than those who now occupy it. In testimony of this, we will refer you to some few passages of scripture. The inhabitants of the heavens, who now reside in the presence of God the Father and his Son Jesus Christ, do not always expect to reside there; they have anticipations as well as we. And they expect to receive another place or location than where they now reside. Have you not read that peculiar passage contained in the 5th chapter of the Revelations, in relation to the inhabitants of heaven? The Revelator John heard

them sing a new and beautiful song, about the unsealing of a
certain book—'Thou art worthy to take the book, and to
open the seals thereof; for thou wast slain and hast redeemed
us to God by thy blood out of every kindred, and tongue, and
people and nation; And hast made us unto our God kings and
priests; and we shall reign on the earth,' etc.

"What! the inhabitants of heaven coming to reign on
this earth? Yes. Some of you may say, 'I should not think
that heavenly people would want to leave the presence of God
and the Lamb, where all is peace and happiness, where there
is no sin to mar the peace of that blessed abode. I should not
suppose that they could anticipate joy in coming back to this
earth.' But the earth is to undergo a change in which it will
be sanctified and made glorious when the sinners are destroyed.
When the Lord performs what I have read to you, namely,
that the inhabitants of the earth are to be burned up, and few
men left; and all the armies of the wicked slaughtered. And
when the prediction of Isaiah is fulfilled that the slain will be
from one end of the earth to the other, and the earth changed
in its position, and a beautiful climate introduced, and all the
dry ground made habitable, and the rough places made smooth,
the valleys raised, and the mountains levelled down, I think
they will then delight to come here. Because this is their old
home, where they once lived. 'Thou hast redeemed us to God
by thy blood out of every kindred, and tongue, and people,
and nation; And hast made us unto our God kings and priests:
and we shall reign on the earth.'

"How will they reign? Will they come here as spiritual
personages without bodies of flesh and bones? No. There will
be a resurrection, and when these great events take place on
the earth, which are so clearly predicted by so many of the
ancient worthies, who held communion with God, the graves
will give up the righteous dead. The saints who were heard
singing that new and beautiful song, even the spirits of the
just, will come from the celestial paradise to claim their resurrected bodies, no more to be subject to death—they will be
immortal and eternal. They will have intelligence in propor
tion to that exalted condition of their spirits and bodies, and

the earth will be adapted to them as a dwelling place. This is the reason why these changes are to take place.

"Geologists say it would take some millions of years to effect any changes of the earth in regard to the location of its continents and islands, and a great number of intelligent readers are inclined to this belief. But there is a God who will disappoint them all, who will show forth his power, causing the earth to rock to and fro, like a drunken man; a God whose power is able to cause the mountains to be cast down and the valleys to come up. When it rains upon the exalted valleys, it will wash down the rich soil upon the rocky mountains which have sunk beneath, making them fertile; and thus the whole surface of the earth will become a fit abode for man in his improved and perfected state, whether immortal or mortal.

" 'Do you think,' one may say, 'there will be mortal beings living on the earth, when these heavenly hosts come?' Yes, and they will dwell together. What, people not subject to sickness, or to sorrow, or punishment, people whose bodies are celestial and immortal, who will endure in their bodies to all eternity! Will they mingle with mortal beings? Yes. Have we any Scripture to sustain us in this? Yes. Our Saviour was immortal when he arose from the tomb, his body of flesh and bones was no longer sensitive to pain; it was a glorified, immortal, and eternal body. Could he mingle with the children of mortality? Yes, for on a certain occasion the Apostles, doubtless thinking the Saviour to be dead, went to their nets, their former pursuit. But Jesus knowing their hearts, went to the sea-shore and there made a fire. By and by he called them to land, and they came. He took a fish and broiled it on the coals, and gave it to them to eat, and he ate with them. He was immortal, they were mortal. Was there any perceptible difference between the appearance of the Saviour on this occasion, and his disciples? No; he did not permit his glory to shine forth, as he did on the Isle of Patmos, when John received his heavenly manifestations. His glory was withheld, and they had no difficulty in looking upon his person.

"I have no doubt there will be a certain degree of the glory of the immortal beings withheld from the children of

[86]

mortality, during the whole period of the millennium. Kings and priests will come here to reign, and will mingle freely among their children of whom they are ancestors. And those who are mortal can receive instruction from those who are immortal, that will prepare them for the time when the earth is to undergo a still greater change. The children of mortality will need this preparation in order to live when this earth is burning up, which is to be its final destiny.

"When Jesus comes, the events that I have named will take place. The earth is destined to pass away; after these immortal beings have dwelt upon it for one thousand years, after Jesus has been here reigning as King of kings and Lord of lords, and people have become familiar with him and all the ancients, by and by the earth will be burned up. You may inquire, 'What is the use of burning it up?' I tell you my reason why I suppose the earth will be burned up. It has been cursed by reason of the fall. In the early ages God said, 'Cursed is the ground for thy sake; in sorrow thou shalt eat of it all the days of thy life.' etc. That curse has not been fully removed to this day, the earth has groaned under wickedness. Its inhabitants have had to suffer all the inclemencies of a rigid climate or the intensities of heat and cold. Millions have thus suffered for many thousands of years, all in consequence of the curse that came upon this creation. This curse is not all to be removed at once, it will be removed, in part, during the Millennium. The curse will not occupy the whole face of the earth to the same extent during that time as it has during the days of wickedness. But so great has been the curse that God decreed that it should suffer death like unto man; it cannot escape it, the change must come, the final change, which is equivalent to death itself. The prophet Isaiah speaks of the earth dying: 'And they that dwell therein shall die in like manner.' As it shall die, so shall all who dwell upon it. When shall it see death? Not until after the Millennium, after the reign of righteousness for the space of one thousand years; after, too, 'the little season,' during which period of time Satan will be loosed out of his prison. It will continue in its temporal state with a portion of the curse upon its face until the devil shall gather together his armies at the end of the thousand years, when he will marshall them, bringing them up on the breadth of the earth, and compassing the camp of the saints and the beloved city. Then the Lord will make the final change; then the last trump will sound, which will bring forth all the sleeping nations; they will come forth with immortal bodies no more to be subject to temporal death. They will come forth from their sleep; tombs and the sea will give up the dead which are in them. The graves of the wicked will be opened, and they will come forth; and a great white throne will appear, as recorded in the 20th chapter of Revelations, and the personage who sits on it is described. Jesus comes then in his glory and power, in a manner far greater than has ever been manifested on this earth before; so great will be the glory of him who sits upon the throne that from before his face the earth and the heaven will flee away, and no place shall be found for them.

"Will not that be a greater change than casting down the mountains, etc., which is to take place at the beginning of the Millennium? The earth is to be burnt by fire, returning to its original elements. It does not say there shall be no place found for the elements, but there shall be no place found for the organized world. Like ourselves, the organization of the mortal body will cease, it will be finally dissolved and the elements of which it is composed will be scattered in space; but that same God that controls the laws by which it exists now will in due time, and when he sees proper, speak to these elements, and by his Almighty power they will again come together, and be formed into a new earth, as is clearly portrayed in the 21st chapter of St. John's Revelations. The apostle not only saw the heaven and the earth pass away, but he saw 'a new heaven and a new earth: for the first heaven and the first earth were passed away.'

"How do you suppose this new earth will be made? Do you suppose the Lord will go away into the immensity of space, and gather together new materials and command them to be organized? No. He will take the same materials, the elements which will have been dissolved by fire, and he will command them again to be reorganized, adapting the resurrected creation to the condition of the inhabitants that will occupy it. It will then be far more glorious than it will appear, during the thousand years of rest; it will then be reorganized by Almighty God in the most perfect form, so that it shall be capable of eternal and everlasting endurance, no more to be dissolved, no more to suffer from the action of the elements one upon the other, as has been the case with this earth during its temporal existence. But it will continue to all eternity, and who are to inhabit it? The saints who have before lived upon it, during the seven thousand years of its temporal existence.

"Have we any account to sustain us in this? Yes, for after John saw the new heaven and new earth, the next thing he tells us of is the population of the new earth. 'And, I John saw the holy city, new Jerusalem, coming down from God out of heaven, prepared as a bride adorned for her husband. And I heard a great voice out of heaven, saying, Behold, the tabernacle of God is with men, and he will dwell with them, and they shall be his people, and God himself shall be with them, and be their God. And God shall wipe away all tears from their eyes, and there shall be no more death, neither sorrow, nor crying, neither shall there be any more pain, for the former things are passed away.'

"The earth then will be made new, immortal, eternal in its nature; and holy beings that John saw come down in this holy city will be its inhabitants. No more death, no more sorrow, etc., in other words, this earth, this creation, will become a heaven. The heavens that exist now are innumerable to man. God has from all eternity been organizing, redeeming and perfecting creations in the immensity of space; all of which, when they are sanctified by celestial law, and made new and eternal, become the abode of the faithful former inhabitants, who also become immortal, through and by celestial law. They are the mansions referred to by the Saviour—'In my Father's house are many mansions.' In other words, we may say, In our Father's dominions are many mansions. They are not like mansions built by man, they are worlds of greater and lesser magnitude. The first grade are exalted, celestial

[89]

bodies, from which celestial light will radiate through the immensity of space.

"We are anxiously praying to dwell in the presence of God the Father, when we depart this life. Where will it be? He will dwell with man upon the earth. Will this confine him to this earth? No, not any more than the kings of the earth are confined to their palaces, or the city in which they may dwell. They have the right to visit the different portions of their dominions and even any parts of the earth. So will God our Eternal Father, when he selects this earth as a habitation, make it as one of his dwelling places, but he will have power to go from one celestial world to another, to visit the myriads of creations, as may seem to him good.

"In thus referring to the changes that the earth must undergo we might ask, Are we living now so as to be prepared for all the dispensations of God's providence? Are we perpared to receive our inheritance upon this earth, when it shall be made eternal? If we keep the celestial law which God shall give to us; or in other words, if we are born first of the water by baptism, and then of the spirit by the baptism of fire and the Holy Ghost, and if we continue to walk in this spirit in newness of life, being new creatures before the Lord our God, and becoming sanctified by the celestial law, even the law of the Gospel, we will then be prepared to inherit this creation, when it shall be made new, and sanctified, and become immortal.

"If we are not thus prepared, where shall we go? God is the author of many creations besides those that are celestial. He will prepare a creation just adapted to the condition of such people—those who are not sanctified by the Gospel in all its fullness, and who do not endure faithful to the end, will find themselves located upon one of the lower creations, where the glory of God will not be made manifest to the same extent. There they will be governed by laws adapted to their inferior capacity and to the condition which they will have plunged themselves in. They will not only suffer after this life, but will fail to receive glory and power and exaltation in the presence of God the Eternal Father; they will fail to receive an everlasting inheritance upon this earth, in its glorified and immortal state. Therefore, how careful the Latter-day Saints should be in order to merit the association of the happy throng whom John heard singing that new song. We desire our inheritance on this earth as well as they. If they could rejoice in anticipation of receiving an inheritance on the earth, how much more can we who know comparatively nothing of the joys of heaven, when our globe will be glorified, a fit habitation for immortal, glorified beings.

"Let us keep the commandments of the Most High; let us so order our lives that we can have a claim upon the Father, looking forward to that period of time when these mortal bodies, which must slumber in the dust, will come forth from the grave, fashioned after the likeness of his most glorious body, to inherit the same glory with him. Amen."

(*Excerpts from discourse delivered on December* 31, 1876)
Journal of Discourses, Vol. 18, *pp.* 318-23.

MARRYING OUTSIDE THE CHURCH

By Orson Pratt

"We cannot feel justified in closing this article on the subject of marriage, without saying a few words to unmarried females in this Church. You will clearly perceive from the revelation which God has given, that you can never obtain a fullness of glory, without being married to a righteous man for time and for all eternity. If you marry a man who receives not the Gospel, you lay a foundation for sorrow in this world, besides losing the society of a husband in eternity. You forfeit your right to an endless increase of immortal lives. And even the children which you may be favored with in this life, will not be entrusted to your charge in eternity, but you will be left in that world, without a husband, without a family, without a kingdom — without any means of enlarging yourselves, being subject to the principalities and powers who are counted worthy of families, and kingdoms and thrones and increase of dominions forever. To them you will be servants and angels—that is, providing that your conduct should be such as to secure this measure of glory. Can it be possible that any females, after knowing these things, will suffer themselves to keep company with persons out of this Church? It matters not how great the morality of such persons may be nor how kind they may be to you, they are not numbered among the people of God, they are not in the way of salvation, they cannot save themselves nor their families, and after what God has revealed upon this subject, you cannot be justified, for one moment, in keeping their company. It would be infinitely better for you to suffer poverty and tribulation with the people of God, than to place yourselves under the power of those who will not embrace the great truths of Heaven. By marrying an unbeliever, you place yourselves in open disobedience to the command of God requiring His people to gather together. Do you expect to be saved in direct violation of the command of Heaven? If not, keep yourselves wholly and entirely from the company of unbelievers. Do you wish the fellowship of the Saints? If you do, have no fellowship for unbelievers. For after the great light which our Father in Heaven has given, none of the Saints will have any confidence in your honesty or sincerity, if you will recklessly throw yourselves away, and cut off all hopes of your future exaltation. No female that has a respect for the work of God, or respect for her future character among his people, will associate or keep company with any but Saints."

Millennial Star, Vol. 15, *p.* 584.

ॐ

INSTRUCTIONS RECEIVED ON HEAVENLY THINGS

By Parley P. Pratt

"In Philadelphia I had the happiness of once more meeting with President Smith, and of spending several days with him and others, and with the Saints in that city and vicinity. During these interviews he taught me many great and glorious principles concerning God and the heavenly order of eternity. It was at this time that I received from him the first idea of eternal family organization, and the eternal union of the sexes in those inexpressibly endearing relationships which none but the highly intellectual, the refined and pure in heart, know how to prize, and which are at the very foundation of everything worthy to be called happiness. Till then I had learned to esteem kindred affections and sympathies as appertaining solely to this transitory state, as something from which the heart must be entirely weaned, in order to be fitted for its heavenly state. It was Joseph Smith who taught me how to prize the endearing relationships of father and mother, husband and wife; of brother and sister, son and daughter. It was from him that I learned that the wife of my bosom might be secured to me for time and all eternity; and that the refined sympathies and affections which endeared us to each other emanated from the foundation of divine eternal love. It was from him that I learned that we might cultivate these affections, and grow and increase in the same to all eternity; while the result of our endless union would be an offspring as numerous as the stars of heaven, or the sands of the sea shore. It was from him that I learned the true dignity and destiny of a son of God, clothed with an eternal priesthood, as the patriarch and sovereign of his countless offspring. It was from him that I learned that the highest dignity of womanhood was to stand as a queen and priestess to her husband, and to reign for ever and ever as the queen mother of her numerous and still increasing offspring.

"I had loved before, but I knew not why. But now I loved with a pureness—an intensity of elevated, exalted feeling, which would lift my soul from the transitory things of this groveling sphere and expand it as the ocean. I felt that God was my heavenly Father indeed; that Jesus was my brother, and that the wife of my bosom was an immortal, eternal companion; a kind ministering angel, given to me as a comfort, and a crown of glory for ever and ever. In short, I could now love with the spirit and with the understanding also. Yet, at that time, my dearly beloved brother, Joseph Smith, had barely touched a single key; had merely lifted a corner of the veil and given me a single glance into eternity."

Autobiography of Parley P. Pratt, pp. 329-330, 1st edition

ॐ

JOSEPH SMITH WAS THE ELIAS, THE RESTORER, THE PRESIDING MESSENGER, HOLDING THE KEYS OF THE "DISPENSATION OF THE FULLNESS OF TIMES"

By PARLEY P. PRATT

"Yes, that extraordinary man, whose innocent blood is yet dripping, as it were, from the hands of assassins and their accessories, in the United States, was the chosen vessel honored of God, and ordained by angels, to ordain other Apostles and Elders, to restore the Church and Kingdom of God, the gifts of the Holy Spirit, and to be a messenger in the spirit and power of Elijah to prepare the way of the Lord! 'For, behold, he will suddenly come to his temple!'

"Like John, who filled a similar mission preparatory to the first advent of the Son of God, he baptized with water unto repentance, for the remission of sins; like him, he was imprisoned; and, like him, his life was taken from the earth; and, finally, like all other true messengers, his message is being demonstrated by its progressive fulfillment,—the powers, gifts, and signs following the administration of his message in all the world, and every minute particular of his predictions fulfilling in the order of events, as the wheels of time bring them due.

"But in one important point his message differs from all former messages. The science of Theology revived by him will never decline, nor its keys be taken from the earth. They are committed to man for the last time. Their consummation will restore the tribes of Israel, and Judah, overthrow all corrupt institutions, usher in the reign of universal peace and

[94]

knowledge, introduce to earth her lawful and eternal king, the crucified Nazarene, the resurrected Messiah, banish darkness and death, sorrow, mourning and tears, from the face of our globe, and crown our race with the laurels of victory and eternal life.

"Ages yet unborn will rise up and call him blessed. A thousand generations of countless myriads will laud his name and recount his deeds, while unnumbered nations bask in the light and enjoy the benefits of the institution founded by his instrumentality.

"His kindred, the nation that gave him birth, and exulted at his death, nay, his very murderers and their posterity, will yet come bending unto him and seek his forgiveness and the benefits of his labors.

"But Oh! the pain! the dark despair! the torments of a guilty conscience! the blackness of darkness in the lower hell, which the guilty wretches will experience before that happy day of deliverance!

"Oh! the countless myriads of the offspring of innocent and honorable men who will walk the earth, tread on the ashes, or plough and reap over the bones and dust of those miserable murderers and their accomplices who have consented to the shedding of innocent blood, ere the final trump shall sound, which calls up their sleeping dust from its long slumbers in the tomb, and their spirits from the prison of the damned!

"And even when this, to them almost interminable, period has rolled away, and they rise from the dead, instead of a welcome exaltation to the presence and society of the sons of God, an eternal banishment awaits them. They never can come where God and Christ dwell, but will be servants in the dominions of the Saints, their former victims."

"The Key to Theology," pp. 80-82, 1938 *edition.*

ह♥

[95]

THE VISION

"IF THE VEIL COULD BE TAKEN FROM OUR EYES"

By Pres. Wilford Woodruff

"If the vail could be taken from our eyes and we could see into the spirit world, we would see that Joseph Smith, Brigham Young and John Taylor had gathered together every spirit that ever dwelt in the flesh in this Church since its organization. We would also see the faithful apostles and elders of the Nephites who dwelt in the flesh in the days of Jesus Christ. In that assembly we would also see Isaiah and every prophet and apostle that ever prophesied of the great work of God. In the midst of those spirits we would see the Son of God, the Savior, who presides and guides and controls the preparing of the kingdom of God on the earth and in heaven. These patriarchs and prophets who have wished for this day, rejoice in the spirit world that the day has come when the Saints of the Most High God have had power to carry out this great mission. * * * * There is a mighty work before this people. The eyes of the dead are upon us. The spirits on the other side rejoice far more than we do, because they know more of what lies before the great work of God in this last dispensation than we do. * * * * The Son of God stands in the midst of that body of celestial spirits, and teaches them their duties concerning the day in which we live, and instructs them what they must do to prepare and qualify themselves to go with him to the earth when he comes to judge every man according to the deeds done in the body. The day is appointed, the hour is appointed, but not revealed, neither to the angels nor to anybody else, but held by the power of God with the Son. These spirits in the heavens will stay and watch over this work till it closes."

Discourse of Pres. Wilford Woodruff, April 7, 1893.

"Here we have four temples, thank the Lord our God! Into those Temples we enter and redeem our dead. We have blessings which have never been given to any other generation since the days of Jesus Christ and the Apostles. The Lord has raised up a people for this purpose. You hold the keys of the

[96]

destiny of your fathers, your mothers, your progenitors, from generation to generation; you hold the keys of their salvation. God has put that power into your hands. But if we do not do what is required of us in this thing, we are under condemnation."

General Conference Report, October, 1897, p. 47.

ॐ

VISION OF THE RESURRECTION OF THE JUST AND UNJUST

By Pres. Wilford Woodruff

"After this my partner left me, and I went alone to Memphis, Tennessee, and met with Brothers Patten and Parrish. After laboring in that part for a length of time, I received a letter from Joseph Smith and Oliver Cowdery in which they requested me to stay in that country and take charge of the churches that we had built up there. The Prophet promised me many things, and said I should lose no blessings by tarrying in that country and doing as he wished me and letting the other brethren go and get their endowments. I was then at the house of Brother Abraham O. Smoot's mother. I received this about sundown. I went into a little room where there was a sofa to pray alone. I felt full of joy and rejoicing at the promises God had made to me through the Prophet. While I was upon my knees praying, my room was filled with light. I looked and a messenger stood by my side. I arose and this personage told me he had come to instruct me. He presented before me a panorama. He told me he wanted me to see with my eyes and understand with my mind what was coming to pass in the earth before the coming of the Son of Man. He commenced with what the revelations say about the sun being turned to darkness, the moon to blood, and the stars falling from heaven. These things were all presented to me one after another, as they will be, I suppose, when they are manifest before the coming of the Son of Man. Then he showed me the

[97]

resurrection of the dead—what is termed the first and second resurrection. In the first resurrection I saw no graves nor anyone raised from the grave. I saw legions of celestial beings, men and women who had received the Gospel all clothed in white robes. In the form they were presented to me, they had already been raised from the grave. After this he showed me what is termed the second resurrection. Vast fields of graves were before me, and the Spirit of God rested upon the earth like a shower of gentle rain, and when that fell upon the graves they were opened, and an immense host of human beings came forth. They were just as diversified in their dress as we are here, or as they were laid down. This personage taught me with regard to these things. Among other things he showed me, there were seven lions like burning brass placed in the heavens. I asked the messenger what they were for. He said they were representative of the different dispensations of the Gospel of Christ to men and they would all be seen in the heavens among the signs that would be shown. After this passed by me, he disappeared. Now, if I had been a painter, I could have drawn everything that I saw. It made an impression upon me that has never left me from that day to this. The next day we had a meeting in the academy. Brother Smoot and some others went with me; but I was a lost man. I hardly knew where I was so enveloped was I in that which I had seen."

(Discourse delivered at the Weber Stake Conference,
Ogden, Monday, October 19, 1896)
Deseret Weekly News, Vol. 53, No. 21, Nov. 7, 1896.

ॐ

APPEARANCE OF THE SIGNERS OF THE DECLARATION OF INDEPENDENCE AND PRESIDENTS OF THE UNITED STATES TO PRESIDENT WILFORD WOODRUFF IN THE ST. GEORGE TEMPLE

"I am going to bear my testimony to this assembly, if I never do it again in my life, that those men who laid the foundation of this American Government and signed the Declaration of Independence were the best spirits the God of Heaven could find on the face of the earth. They were choice spirits, not wicked men. General Washington and all the men that labored for the purpose were inspired of the Lord. Another thing I am going to say here, because I have a right to say it. Every one of those men that signed the Declaration of Independence with General Washington called upon me, as an Apostle of the Lord Jesus Christ, in the Temple at St. George, two consecutive nights, and demanded at my hands that I should go forth and attend to the ordinances of the house of God for them. Men are here, I believe, that know of this—Brothers J. D. T. McAllister, David H. Cannon and James C. Bleak. Brother McAllister baptized me for all these men, and I then told these brethren that it was their duty to go into the Temple and labor until they got endowments for all of them. They did it. Would those spirits have called upon me, as an Elder in Israel, to perform that work if they had not been noble spirits before God? They would not. I bear this testimony because it is true. The spirit of God bore record to myself and the brethren while we were laboring in that way." * * *

"Every father and mother has a great responsibility resting upon them, to redeem their dead. Do not neglect it. You will have sorrow if you do. Any man will, who neglects the redemption of his dead that he has power to officiate for here. When you get to the other side of the veil, if you have entered into these Temples and redeemed your progenitors by the ordinances of the House of God, you will hold the keys of their redemption from eternity to eternity. Do not neglect this! God bless you. Amen."

(Report of President Wilford Woodruff, General Conference, April 10, 1898, pp. 89-90.)

ह≫

[99]

THE VISION

TESTIMONY OF PRESIDENT WILFORD WOODRUFF CONTINUED

"We have labored in the St. George Temple since January, and we have done all we could there; and the Lord has stirred up our minds, and many things have been revealed to us concerning the dead. President Young has said to us, and it is verily so, if the dead could they would speak in language loud as ten thousand thunders, calling upon the servants of God to rise up and build Temples, magnify their calling and redeem their dead. This doubtless sounds strange to those present who believe not the faith and doctrine of the Latter-day Saints; but when we get to the spirit world we will find out that all that God has revealed is true. We will find, too, that everything there is reality, and that God has a body, parts and passions, and the erroneous ideas that exist now with regard to him will have passed away. I feel to say little else to the Latter-day Saints wherever and whenever I have the opportunity of speaking to them, than to call upon them to build these Temples now under way, to hurry them up to completion. The dead will be after you, they will seek after you as they have after us in St. George. They called upon us, knowing that we held the keys and power to redeem them.

"I will here say, before closing, that two weeks before I left St. George, the spirits of the dead gathered around me, wanting to know why we did not redeem them. Said they: 'You have had the use of the Endowment House for a number of years and yet nothing has ever been done for us. We laid the foundation of the government you now enjoy, and we never apostatized from it, but we remained true to it and were faithful to God.' These were the signers of the Declaration of Independence, and they waited on me for two days and two nights. I thought it very singular that notwithstanding so much work had been done, and yet nothing had been done for them. The thought never entered my heart, from the fact, I suppose, that heretofore our minds were reaching after our more immediate friends and relatives. I straightway went into the baptismal font and called upon Brother McAllister to baptize me for the signers of the Declaration of Independence, and fifty other eminent men, making one hundred in all, including John Wesley, Columbus, and others; I then baptized him for every President of the United States except three; and when their cause is just, somebody will do the work for them."

(Remarks made at General Conference, Sept. 16, 1877.)
Journal of Discourses, Vol. 19, p. 229.

ॐ

VISITATIONS OF JOSEPH THE PROPHET TO PRESIDENT WILFORD WOODRUFF

"One morning, while we were at Winter Quarters, Brother Brigham Young said to me and the brethren that he had a visitation the night previous from Joseph Smith. I asked him what he said to him. He replied that Joseph had told him to tell the people to labor to obtain the Spirit of God; that they needed that to sustain them and to give them power to go through their work on the earth. * * *

"Now I will give you a little of my experience in this line. Joseph Smith visited me a great deal after his death, and taught me many important principles. The first time* he visited me was while I was in a storm at sea. I was going on my last mission to preside in England. My companions were Brother Leonard W. Hardy, Brother Milton Holmes, Brother Dan Jones and another brother and my wife and two other women. We had been traveling three days and nights in a heavy gale and were being driven backwards. Finally I asked my companions to come into the cabin with me, and I told them to pray that the Lord would change the wind. I had no fears of being lost; but I did not like the idea of being driven back to New York, as I wanted to go on my journey. We all offered the same prayer, both men and women; and when we got through we stepped on to the deck and in less than a minute

---

*Erroneously quoted "last" time in original report.

it was as though a man had taken a sword and cut that gale through, and you might have thrown a muslin handkerchief out and it would not have moved it. The night following this, Joseph and Hyrum visited me, and the Prophet laid before me a great many things. Among other things he told me to get the Spirit of God; that all of us needed it. He also told me what the Twelve Apostles would be called to go through on the earth before the coming of the Son of Man, and what the reward of their labors would be; but all that was taken from me for some reason. Nevertheless I know it was most glorious although much would be required at our hands.

"Joseph Smith continued visiting myself and others up to a certain time, and then it stopped. The last time I saw him was in heaven. In the night vision I saw him at the door of the temple in heaven. He came and spoke to me. He said he could not stop to talk with me because he was in a hurry. The next man I met was Father Smith; he could not talk with me because he was in a hurry. I met a half a dozen brethren who had held high positions on earth and none of them could stop to talk with me because they were in a hurry. I was much astonished. By and by I saw the Prophet again, and I got the privilege to ask him a question. 'Now,' said I, 'I want to know why you are in a hurry. I have been in a hurry all through my life but I expected my hurry would be over when I got into the kingdom of heaven, if I ever did.' Joseph said, 'I will tell you, Brother Woodruff, every dispensation that has had the Priesthood on the earth and has gone into the celestial kingdom, has had a certain amount of work to do to prepare to go to the earth with the Savior when He goes to reign on the earth. Each dispensation has had ample time to do this work. We have not. We are the last dispensation, and so much work has to be done and we need to be in a hurry in order to accomplish it.' Of course, that was satisfactory with me, but it was new doctrine to me."

(Discourse delivered by President Wilford Woodruff at the Weber Stake Conference, Ogden, Monday, October 19, 1896.)
Deseret Weekly News, Vol. 53, No. 21

"THE SON OF MAN WILL COME TO THE SAINTS WHILE IN THE ROCKY MOUNTAINS" —JOSEPH THE PROPHET

"I arrived in Kirtland on Saturday (1833) and there met Joseph and Hyrum Smith in the street. I was introduced to Joseph Smith. It was the first time that I had ever seen him in my life. He invited me home to spend the Sabbath with him, and I did so. They had meeting on Sunday.

"On Sunday night the Prophet called on all who held the Priesthood to gather into the little log school house they had there. It was a small house, perhaps 14 feet square. But it held the whole of the Priesthood of the Church of Jesus Christ of Latter-day Saints who were then in the town of Kirtland, and who had gathered together to go off in Zion's Camp. That was the first time I ever saw Oliver Cowdery, or heard him speak; the first time I ever saw Brigham Young and Heber C. Kimball, and the two Pratts, and Orson Hyde and many others. There were no Apostles in the Church then except Joseph Smith and Oliver Cowdery. When we got together the Prophet called upon the Elders of Israel with him to bear testimony of this work. Those that I have named spoke and a good many that I have not named, bore their testimonies. When they got through the Prophet said: 'Brethren, I have been very much edified and instructed in your testimonies here tonight, but I want to say to you before the Lord, that you know no more concerning the destinies of this Church and Kingdom than a babe upon its mother's lap. You don't comprehend it.' I was rather surprised. He said: 'It is only a little handful of Priesthood you see here tonight, but this Church will fill North and South America—it will fill the world.' Among other things he said: 'It will fill the Rocky Mountains. There will be tens of thousands of Latter-day Saints who will be gathered in the Rocky Mountains and there they will open the door for the establishing of the Gospel among the Lamanites who will receive the Gospel and their endowments, and the blessings of God. This people will go into the Rocky Mountains; they will

there build Temples to the Most High. They will raise up a
posterity there, and the Latter-day Saints who dwell in these
mountains will stand in the flesh until the coming of the Son
of Man. The son of Man will come to them while in the
Rocky Mountains'."

(Remarks of President Wilford Woodruff)
General Conference Report, April 8, 1898, p. 57.

ह৯

VISION OF THE REDEMPTION OF THE DEAD
By PRESIDENT JOSEPH F. SMITH

"As I pondered over these things which are written, (1
Peter 3:18-20; II Peter 4:6) the eyes of my understanding were
opened, and the Spirit of the Lord rested upon me, and I saw
the hosts of the dead, both small and great. And there were
gathered together in one place an innumerable company of the
spirits of the just, who had been faithful in the testimony of
Jesus while they lived in mortality, and who had offered sacrifice in the similitude of the great sacrifice of the Son of God,
and had suffered tribulation in their Redeemer's name. All
these had departed the mortal life, firm in the hope of a glorious
resurrection, through the grace of God the Father and his Only
Begotten Son, Jesus Christ.

"I beheld that they were filled with joy and gladness, and
were rejoicing together because the day of their deliverance
was at hand. They were assembled awaiting the advent of the
Son of God into the spirit world, to declare their redemption
from the bands of death. Their sleeping dust was to be restored unto its perfect frame, bone to his bone, and the sinews
and the flesh upon them, the spirit and the body to be united
never again to be divided, that they might receive a fulness of
joy.

"While this vast multitude waited and conversed, rejoicing in the hour of their deliverance from the chains of death,
the Son of God appeared, declaring liberty to the captives who
had been faithful, and there he preached to them the everlasting
gospel, the doctrine of the resurrection and the redemption of

[104]

mankind from the fall, and from individual sins on conditions of repentance. But unto the wicked he did not go, and among the ungodly and the unrepentant who had defiled themselves while in the flesh, his voice was not raised, neither did the rebellious who rejected the testimonies and the warnings of the ancient prophets behold his presence, nor look upon his face. Where these were, darkness reigned, but among the righteous there was peace, and the saints rejoiced in their redemption, and bowed the knee and acknowledged the Son of God as their Redeemer and Deliverer from death and the chains of hell. Their countenances shone and the radiance from the presence of the Lord rested upon them and they sang praises unto his holy name.

"I marveled, for I understood that the Savior spent about three years in His ministry among the Jews and those of the house of Israel, endeavoring to teach them the everlasting gospel and call them unto repentance; and yet, notwithstanding His mighty works and miracles and proclamation of the truth in great power and authority, there were but few who hearkened to his voice and rejoiced in his presence and received salvation at his hands. But his ministry among those who were dead was limited to the brief time intervening between the crucifixion and his resurrection; and I wondered at the words of Peter wherein he said that the Son of God preached unto the spirits in prison who sometime were disobedient, when once the longsuffering of God waited in the days of Noah, and how it was possible for him to preach to those spirits and perform the necessary labor among them in so short a time.

"And as I wondered, my eyes were opened, and my understanding quickened, and I perceived that the Lord went not in person among the wicked and the disobedient who had rejected the truth, to teach them; but behold, from among the righteous he organized his forces and appointed messengers, clothed with power and authority, and commissioned them to go forth and carry the light of the gospel to them that were in darkness, even to all the spirits of men. And thus was the gospel preached to the dead. And the chosen messengers went forth to declare the acceptable day of the Lord, and proclaim liberty to the captives who were bound; even unto all who would repent of their sins and receive the gospel. Thus was the gospel preached to those who had died in their sins, without a knowledge of the truth, or in transgression, having rejected the prophets. These were taught faith in God, repentance from sin, vicarious baptism for the remission of sins, the gift of the Holy Ghost by the laying on of hands, and all other principles of the gospel that were necessary for them to know in order to qualify themselves that they might be judged according to men in the flesh, but live according to God in the spirit."*

Improvement Era, Vol. 22, p. 166.

ह‍०

REDEMPTION BEYOND THE GRAVE

By PRESIDENT JOSEPH F. SMITH

"In relation to the deliverance of spirits from their prison house, of course, we believe that can only be done after the gospel has been preached to them in the spirit, and they have accepted the same, and the work necessary to their redemption by the living, be done for them. That this work may be hastened so that all who believe in the spirit world may receive the benefit of deliverance, it is revealed that the great work of the Millennium shall be the work in the temples for the redemption of the dead; and then, we hope to enjoy the benefits of revelation through the Urim and Thummim, or by such means as the Lord may reveal concerning those for whom the work shall be done, so that we may not work by chance, or by faith alone, without knowledge, but with the actual knowledge revealed unto us. It stands to reason that, while the gospel may be preached unto all, the good and the bad, or rather those who would repent and those who would not

---

*This Vision of the Redemption of the Dead was submitted, October 31, 1918, to the Counsellors in the First Presidency, the Council of the Twelve and the Patriarch, and by them unanimously accepted.

repent in the spirit world, the same as it is here, redemption will only come to those who repent and obey. There is, no doubt, great leniency given to people who are anxious to do the work for their dead and, in some instances, very unworthy people may have the work done for them; it does not follow, however, that they will receive any benefit therefrom, and the correct thing is to do the work only for those of whom we have the testimony that they will receive it. However, we are disposed to give the benefit of the doubt to the dead, as it is better to do the work for many who are unworthy than to neglect one who is worthy. Now, we know in part, and see in part, but we steadfastly look forward to the time when that which is perfect will come. We are left largely to our own agency here, to exercise our own intelligence, and to receive all the light that is revealed, so far as we are capable of receiving it; and only those who seek the light, and desire it, are likely to find it."

Editorial in Improvement Era, Vol. 5, pp. 146-7.

ಠ

THE WIDER HOPE — IF A MAN DIES IN UN-BELIEF, INDIFFERENCE OR DISOBEDIENCE MAY HE BE SAVED?

By ELDER NEPHI L. MORRIS

(A Series of Four Discourses—See Deseret News for June 1, 8, 15, 22, 1935)

I.

Text: "But Jesus answered them: . . . Verily, verily, I say unto you, the hour is coming, and now is, when the dead shall hear the voice of the Son of God; and they that hear shall live.

". . . Marvel not at this; for the hour is coming in which all that are in the graves shall hear his voice, and shall come forth; they that have done good, unto the resurrection of life; and they that have done evil, unto the resurrection of damnation." (John 5:25, 28, 29.)

THE VISION

"This is the first of four addresses dealing with the subject of "The Wider Hope, or a Salvation Provided for the Dead."

The Latter-day Saints claim that the Church of Jesus Christ is again established upon the earth in its perfection; that every power and authority, ordinance, and principle, essential to the complete salvation and exaltation of man is possessed by the Church. The process of complete restoration and reestablishment was accomplished through a period of years. First came the revelation of God; then the revelation of the Book of Mormon and its translation by the gift and power of God. Then came the restoration of the Priesthood of Aaron, and the authority to minister in the preparatory gospel, namely, of Repentance and Baptism by immersion for the remission of sins. Immediately following came the keys and powers of Apostleship and the fullness of Priesthood. This was properly followed by the setting up of the Church in its perfect form, with the Presiding High Priests, Patriarchs, Apostles, Seventies, Elders, and the Orders of the Lesser Priesthood.

In addition to these important powers, specific Dispensations and Keys were restored to the earth, such as the Keys of Gathering, which were first held by Moses in the exercise of which he gathered the children of Israel out of Egypt to their Land of Promise. And from the Prophet Elijah, Joseph Smith received the Keys of the Priesthood that pertain to a salvation for the dead. The promise was made that Elijah would come and establish in the hearts of the children a desire to work for the salvation and exaltation of their fathers. This promise was made by the Prophet Malachi, with the assurance that it was to occur "before the great and dreadful day of the Lord." Through the exercise of this key the Latter-day Saints have received the spirit of Elijah and the understanding of the Gospel of Jesus Christ, by means of which its saving powers may be extended into the Spirit World. Thereby the living officiate in the ordinances of the Gospel for and in behalf of the dead. The ordinances thus performed are made available to those who have died in impenitence or unbelief, or in complete ignorance of the Gospel. Through the preaching of the

[108]

Gospel in the Spirit World, such spirits as here described may accept its teachings and "live according to God in the spirit" by yielding obedience to the Gospel. When conversion shall have come to them, the ordinances of baptism and the laying on of hands, ordinations and sealings, will be available for them if properly performed upon the earth, through the administration of the Keys and Powers of this Priesthood. This is the work commonly known among Latter-day Saints as "salvation of the dead." Such a salvation is obviously a necessity if the Church of Christ be the institution intended to compass the almost universal salvation of the race. The possession of this power, and the knowledge of this principle and the ordinances connected therewith, establish convincingly the fact of the restoration to the earth of the gospel in its fulness. No other Christian Church lays claim to the possession of these keys and authorities, or even of a knowledge of the principle of salvation for the dead. The absence of these things in all other churches for a period of nearly two thousand years, is to us, an overwhelming evidence of the falling away from the primitive faith, and hence, the necessity of a restoration in its original fulness.

For the purpose of comparing the new light that has come into the world in our day, with the limited light of the past, and the knowledge and understanding now upon the earth in contrast with the confusion and ignorance of the Gospel in past centuries, and in comparison of the love of God and the mercy of Christ as expressed in the Gospel with the prejudice and narrow-mindedness of mankind, we shall review the teachings of the Christian World on the important subject involved in this question, namely, the state of the souls of men after death and the possibilities of salvation which the gospel provides for them. We shall also consider the meaning of the terms "hell," "damnation," and "endless punishment," and the hope of redemption from the unhappy state of the unbelieving, or disobedient, in the spirit world.

In a general sense, we may with one statement, dispose of all protestant churches, with respect to this subject as none of them has ever laid claim to any such principle of belief as a salvation for the dead. (Some have deeply felt the need of it.) None of them has ever taught the doctrine herein set forth. Nor have they a provisional ordinance of the Gospel for that purpose. It is true, however, as we shall later bring to light in this discussion, that a small group of glorious men of the Anglican church did courageously announce their belief in the "wider hope," and in so doing almost lost their standing among their fellow religionists.

The Catholic is the only church excepting its alienated sister, the Greek Orthodox church, that holds to a belief that in any way resembles the principle of salvation for the dead. But it has so limited a conception of the principle as such, that we are not warranted in regarding their belief as being of the same proportions as the definitely developed doctrine of salvation beyond the grave. We will perceive, however, that the teachings of the Roman Catholic church, as set forth by their accepted authorities alone approach in some degree, this great Christian principle of Salvation for the departed. The claims of the Roman Catholic church with respect to church integrity and divine authority, are in every respect equal to those of the Latter-day Saints. They may even be more positive and sweeping, if it were possible. They unmistakably make higher claims in respect to administrative infallibility and the superlative perfection of their church. One of the latest expressions of the Catholic church on this subject, may be found in the Encyclical of Pius XI, issued January 6, 1928. It reads: "First, the perfection of the Catholic religion as a system of doctrine and practice. It has been defined with increasing clearness and rigidity through the centuries, in reply to the attacks of heretics or to meet other emergencies, that the system itself is supernaturally perfect, and is now exactly what it was when it was first revealed by Christ, and what it must always be. The Roman Catholic church, therefore, has nothing to learn from any other source. It cannot compromise, confer, or co-operate, where such action would cast any doubt upon its assurance of its own perfection.

"Second, the infallibility of the visible church as the agency to which God has entrusted the preservation, definition, administration, and propagation of that perfect system; and specifically in the infallibility of the pope as the head of the church, and the personal representative of Christ.

"Third, the authority of the church over its own members in all matters which it defines as related to faith and morals, and its inherent right to exercise all the powers and functions, temporal as well as spiritual, which in its own infallible judgment, are necessary to the discharge of the duties enumerated above."

With the position of the Catholic church thus defined, there remains no ground for doubt as to its claims of completeness, fulness, and even a supernatural perfection. We might observe that with the all-sufficient attitude which the church deliberately justifies itself in assuming, if it were lacking any principle of faith, or any ordinance essential to the salvation of the souls of men, there would be no hope for such a deficiency ever being supplied because it has "nothing to learn from any other source."

The only teaching authorized by the Roman church which bears a semblance to the principle of salvation for the dead, is that which is defined by Cardinal Gibbons, and other like authorities of the church under the heading of "Purgatory" and it consists of nothing more than prayers for the dead.

We here quote the cardinal:

"The Catholic church teaches that, besides a place of eternal torments for the wicked and of everlasting rest for the righteous, there exists in the next life a middle state of temporary punishment, allotted for those who have died in venial sins (i. e., excusable, slight, trivial, N. L. M.)., or who have not satisfied the justice of God for sins already forgiven. She also teaches us that although the souls consigned to this intermediate state, commonly called purgatory, cannot help themselves, (can they not repent? N. L. M.) they may be aided by the suffrages of the faithful on earth. The existence of purgatory naturally implies the correlative dogma—the utility of praying for the dead; for, the souls consigned to this middle state have not reached the terms of their journey. They are still exiles from heaven, and fit subjects for divine clemency."

THE VISION

"Is it not strange that this cherished doctrine should also be called in question by the levelling innovators of the sixteenth century, (i. e., the reformers, N. L. M.), when we consider that it is clearly taught in the Old Testament: that it is, at least, insinuated in the New Testament; that it is unanimously proclaimed by the Fathers of the church; that it is embodied in all the ancient liturgies of the Oriental and the western church; and that it is a doctrine alike consonant with our reason, and eminently consoling to the human heart.

"1. It is a doctrine plainly contained in the Old Testament and piously practised by the Hebrew people. At the close of an engagement which Judas Maccabeus had with the enemy, he orders prayers and sacrifices to be offered up for his slain comrades. And making a gathering, he sent twelve thousand drachms of silver to Jerusalem for sacrifice to be offered for the sins of the dead, thinking well and religiously concerning the resurrection. For, if he had not hoped that they that were slain should rise again, it would have seemed superfluous and vain to pray for the dead. * * * It is, therefore, a holy and wholesome thought to pray for the dead, that they may be loosed from sins."

* * *

"You now pereceive that this devotion is not an invention of modern times, but a doctrine universally enforced in the first and purest ages of the church.

"You see that praying for the dead was not a devotion cautiously recommended by some obscure or visionary writer, but an act of religion preached and inculcated by all the great doctors and fathers of the church, who are the recognized expounders of the Christian religion."

And it might be interesting to observe in passing, that Father Di Bruno in his short and simple exposition of Catholic doctrine, among other set and formal prayers, gives one for the dead and another for a departed father and mother and still another for the faithful departed.

It might also be observed that Catholic authorities appeal to ancient authorities of the Old and the New Testament, the Apocrypha and the early Christian fathers for sanction and approval of this well-established practice of praying for the release from purgatory of the sin-retarded dead. There is not a single, straight-forward declaration that even hints at so substantial a principle as the vicarious administration of the ordinance of baptism for the departed. I have not found in their teachings under this heading a single allusion to the reference which the Apostle Paul made to the Corinthian Church in which he mentions specifically the matter of baptism for the dead. The ordinance is obviously not accepted or countenanced by them in connection with the departed. Yet the sacrament of baptism is held to be a necessity to all souls living on earth if they wish to be born into the Father's Kingdom.

Cardinal Gibbons says further: "During my sojourn in Rome at the Ecumenical Council, I devoted a great deal of my leisure time to the examination of the various liturgies of the schismatic churches of the east. I found in all of them formulas of prayers for the dead almost identical with that of the Roman Missal. 'Remember: Oh Lord, thy servants who are gone before us, with the sign of faith, and sleep in peace. To these, Oh Lord, and to all who rest in Christ grant, we beseech Thee, a place of refreshment, light, and peace, through the name of Jesus Christ, Our Lord'." The cardinal further assures us "that the Oriental Patriarchs and Bishops in communion with the See of Rome, who belonged to the Armenian, Chaldean, and Coptic, the Maronite, and Syriac churches, assured him that the schismatic Christians of the east among whom they lived, have, without exception, prayers and sacrifices for the dead."

In explanation of this beautiful religious practice, the cardinal asks the question: "If your brother dies with some slight strains upon his soul, a sin of impatience, for instance, or an idle word, is he fit to enter heaven with these blemishes upon his soul? No, the sanctity of God forbids it. For nothing defiled shall enter the kingdom of heaven. Will you consign him for these minor transgressions to eternal torments with adulterers and murderers. No, the justice and mercy of God forbid it. Therefore your common sense demands a middle place of expiation for the purgation of the soul, before it is worthy of enjoying the companionship of God and his Saints. God 'will render to every man according to his works'—to the pure and unsullied, everlasting bliss; to the reprobate, eternal damnation; to the soul stained with minor faults, a place of purgation.

This doctrine relating to a "middle place" is made plain in the teachings of the Book of Mormon. The Prophet Alma says, "There is a space between death and the resurrection of the body, and a state of the soul in happiness or in misery, until the time which is appointed of God when the dead shall come forth, and be re-united both soul and body, and be brought to stand before God, and be judged according to their works."

". . . But, behold, an awful death cometh upon the wicked; for they die as to the things pertaining to righteousness, for they are unclean, and no unclean thing can inherit the Kingdom of God; but they are cast out, and consigned to partake of the fruits of their labors, or their works, which have been evil, and they drink the dregs of a bitter cup."

It will be observed that the Catholic doctrine advocates prayers for the dead who have accepted Christ, and yet are guilty of minor sins. It nowhere throws out any hope whatsoever, as I read their teachings, of admittance into the Church of the First Born, of those who were in their earthly lives unconverted and sinful, but says that the reprobate shall endure eternal damnation. Neither does it appear that the Catholic teaching offers any means of initiation into the Church of those who have died in innocent ignorance, or in willful disobedience of Christ. The practice, beautiful as it is and filled with spirituality and love, does not in any appreciable degree seem to meet the needs of that larger salvation which was unquestionably the hope and mission of the church from before the foundations of the earth, viz., the ultimate, well-nigh universal salvation of mankind. Such was undoubtedly the looked-for triumph of the Church suggested in the declaration "that at the name of Jesus, every knee should bow . . . and that every tongue should confess that Jesus Christ is Lord to the glory of God, the Father." Such confession of faith, or acknowledgment of Christ does not necessarily imply a universal exaltation in the higher degrees of glory. Only the true and tried, and valiant, shall attain to such glory. Others, if honorable and conscientious, may attain to a salvation fitting their merits and capacities.

II.

Leaving the Catholic church, somewhat, and going now to the Protestant churches, let us consider their teachings with respect to the conditions surrounding the souls of men after death, as well as their teachings concerning "Hell" and "Endless Punishment." Deans Farrar and Plumptre have given us the benefit of their wide reading upon this subject. In a sermon preached in Westminster Abbey, November 11, 1877, Farrar said: "What the popular notion of hell is, you are well aware. Many of us were scared with it, horrified with it, perhaps almost maddened by it in our childhood. It is that, the moment a human being dies—at whatever age, under whatever disadvantages—his fate is sealed finally and forever; and that if he die in unrepented sin, that fate is a NEVER ENDING AGONY, amid physical tortures the most frightful that can be imagined; so that, when we think of the future of the human race, we must conceive of a vast and burning prison in which the lost souls of millions and millions rise and shriek forever, tormented in a flame that never will be quenched. You have only to read the Manuals, you have only to study the pictures published, though but rarely by members of our own Church, and more frequently by some Roman Catholics on the one hand, and some sections of Non-Conformists on the other, to see that such has been, and is, the common belief of Christendom." In a footnote Dean Farrar observes, "That many of the ablest and most thoughtful Non-Conformists— especially among the vigorous and independent and eloquent ministers—have rejected the dogma of endless agony for all who die in sin." He says that the Roman Catholic priests and Non-Conformist ministers, being less highly educated than the Anglican clergy, have some very horrible inventions about hell, but is free to admit that for the Roman Catholics the present and immediate horror of hell is very greatly mitgated, and even to some degree dispelled, by the doctrine of purgatory.

We are quite sure that hell was never more fearfully depicted by any minister than by the ardent American theologian, Jonathan Edwards. In his pictures of hell he displayed an unsurpassed genius for imagination of the lurid. Listen to this as a sample of medieval misconception of the state of the souls of men after death: "The world will probably be converted into a great lake or liquid globe of fire, in which the wicked shall be overwhelmed, which shall always be in tempest, in which they shall be tossed to and fro, having no rest day or night, vast waves or billows of fire continually rolling over their heads, of which they shall ever be full from a quick sense within, and without; their heads, their eyes, their tongues, their hands, their feet, their loins, their vitals, shall forever be full of a glowing melting fire, enough to melt the very rocks and elements."

"Also they shall be full of the most quick and lively sense to feel the torments, not to say millions of ages, but forever and ever without any end at all." Even the sublime poet Milton, employed his genius in describing with frightful sentences, the sufferings of the wicked: "Who shall be thrown down eternally into the deepest and darkest gulf of hell under the despiteful control, the trample and spoil of all the other damned, and in anguish and torture, shall have no other ease than to exercise a raving and bestial tyranny over them as their slaves and negroes, and shall remain in that plight forever, the basest, the lowermost, the most dejected, most underfoot and down trodden vassals of perdition."

And Bishop Jeremy Taylor, allows his imagination to revel in the burning tortures, which he pours over his lurid page in these words: "For though in hell the accursed souls shall have no more than they deserve, and there are not these over-running measures as there are in heaven, and therefore that the joys of heaven are infinitely greater joys than the pains of hell are great pains, yet even these are a full measure of a full iniquity, pain above patience, sorrow without ease, amazement without consideration, despair without the intervals of a little hope, indignation without the possession of any good; there dwells envy and confusion, disorder and sad remembrances, perpetual wolves and continuous shrieking, uneasiness and all the evils of the soul." St. Augustine dared to say that infants dying unbaptized would certainly be damned. And Farrar observes that "due mainly to the authority of St. Augustine, which was in many respects so disastrous, the entire medieval Church held the doctrine of the damnation of infants dying unbaptized." In the "Articles to Establish Christian Quietness" in 1536, it was laid down that infants dying in their infancy shall undoubtedly be saved by the Sacrament of baptism, "and else not." Happily those three words were later rescinded.

In the "Inferno," Dante describes himself as being led by his guide (Virgil) in the deep descent into Limbo, which is the first circle of hell, "where he finds the souls of those who, though they have lived virtuously, and have not to suffer for great sins, nevertheless, through lack of baptism, merit not the bliss of Paradise." Hence he is led on by Virgil to descend into the second circle. Speaking of the condition of those in Limbo the poet proceeds:

> "Here as mine ear could note, no plaint was heard
> Except of sighs, that made the eternal air
> Tremble, not caused by tortures, but by grief
> Felt by those multitudes, many and vast,
> Or men, women, and infants. Then to me
> The gentle guide: 'Inquirest thou not what spirits
> Are these which thou beholdest? Ere thou pass
> Farther, I would thou know, that these of sin
> Were blameless; and if aught they merited.
> It profits not, since baptism was not theirs,
> The portal of thy faith. If they before
> The Gospel lived, they served not God aright;
> And among such am I. For these defects,
> And for no other evil, we are lost;
> Only so far afflicted, that we live
> Desiring without hope.' Sore grief assailed
> My heart at hearing this, for well I knew
> Suspended in that Limbo many a soul
> Of mighty worth."
> "O, tell me, sire revered!
> Tell me, my Master, I began through wish
> Of full assurance in that holy faith
> Which vanquishes all error; 'say did e'er
> Any, or through his own or other's merit,
> Come forth hence, who afterward was blest?'

THE VISION

Piercing the secret import of my speech,
He answer'd: 'I was new to this estate,
When I beheld a puissant one arrive
Amongst us, with victorious trophy crown'd.
He forth the shade of our first parent drew.
Abel, his child, and Noah, righteous man,
Of Moses lawgiver for faith approved,
Of Patriarch Abraham, and David king,
Israel with his sire and with his sons,
Nor without Rachel whom so hard he won,
And others many more, whom he to bliss
Exalted. Before these be thou assured,
No spirit of humankind was ever saved."

St. Thomas of Equinium, yielded to the same fantastic reasoning as he taught that the bliss of the saved "may be all the more keen because they are permitted to gaze on the punishment of the wicked." Jonathan Edwards, never failing in ghastly imagination, says: "That the damned shall be tormented in the presence of the Holy Angels and in the presence of the Lamb, so will they be tormented in the presence of the glorified Saints. Hereby the Saints will be made more sensible how great their salvation is. The view of the misery of the damned will double the ardor of the love and gratitude of Saints in heaven." Volumes of this kind of inhuman and un-Christian teachings are available. We turn from them, sickened and appalled, and employ the comments of Cannon Farrar on such horrifying teachings to express our feelings and judgment on the subject: "What a world, we may well exclaim, for the loving and merciful eyes of God to contemplate! How frightful a result! In spite of how infinite a sacrifice! And we are taught that one instant makes all the difference between a poor, frail, sinful soul, over which its Savior yearns, for which the spirit pleads, which God, its Father and Creator, loves with an infinite tenderness, and a lost, accursed, shrieking, blaspheming, ever—never—dying son of endless and irretrievable perdition. This is what the popular, the common view, has a thousand times asserted and still profess to assert! And is this the Gospel? Are these the "Glad Tidings of Great Joy?" Farrar further says: "I repudiate these crude and glaring travesties of the awful and holy will of God; I arraign them as ignorantly merciless. I impeach them as a falsehood against Christ's Universal and absolute redemption! I denounce them as a blasphemy against God's exceeding and eternal love."

Addressing his class with a personal appeal this great-hearted, Christ-loving man demanded, "Now I ask you, my brethren, where would be these popular teachings about hell— the kind of teachings which I have quoted to you, and de-scribed—if we calmly and deliberately, by substituting the true translation, erased from our English Bibles, as being inadequate or erroneous, or disputed renderings, the three words, 'dam-nation,' 'hell,' and 'everlasting.' Yet I say unhesitatingly, I say, claiming the fullest right to speak on this point, I say, with the calmest and most unflinching sense of responsibility—I say, standing here in the sight of God, and of my Savior, and it may be of the angels, and spirits of the dead—that not one of those three expressions ought to stand any longer in our English Bible, and that being—in our present acceptation of them, in the notion (that is) which all uneducated persons attach to them—simply mistranslations, they most unquestion-ably will not stand unexplained in the revised version of the Bible if the revisers have understood their duty. (The R. V., 1884, renders 'damned' 'condemned,' N. L. M.) The verb 'to damn' in Greek testament is neither more nor less than the verb 'to condemn' and the words translated 'damnation' are simply the words, which, in the vast majority of instances, the same translators have translated, and rightly translated, by 'judgment' and condemnation. The word sometimes trans-lated 'everlasting' is simply the word which, in its first sense applied to things which have utterly and long since passed away; and is in its second, sense something spiritual, something means, 'age-long' or 'aeonian' and which is in the Bible itself above and beyond time—as when the knowledge of God is said to be Eternal Life."

In the support of his position, Dean Farrar, quotes from his own article in Dr. Smith's Dictionary of the Bible, where he defines the term "Hell," by saying: "There is no everlasting damnation, according to the Talmud; there is only a temporary punishment even for the worst sinners." He also refers to the Jewish Chronicle, where the editor, generally believed to be a learned Talmudist, emphatically declares in recent numbers, that Endless Torment has never been taught by the Rabbis as a doctrine of the Jewish Church. He concludes his lecture by using the answer of Thomas Erskine, that "we are lost here as much as there, and that Christ came to seek and to save the lost, and my hope is, that the vast majority at any rate, of the lost, may at length be found." . . . "Have faith in God. There is hope for you;—hope for you even if death overtake you before the final victory is won;—hope for the poor in spirit, for their's is the kingdom of heaven;—hope for the mourners, for they shall be comforted;—though you too may have to be purified, in that Gehanna, of Aeonian fire beyond the grave . . . that there will be a restitution of all things;—that God will not that any should perish;—that Christ both died, and rose, and revived, that he might be Lord both of the dead and the living;—that as in Adam all die, even so in Christ shall all be made alive."

In Dean Farrar's introduction to his "Eternal Hope," published in 1877, he says: "I come to a word, translated rightly and frequently 'Eternal' and wrongly and unnecessarily 'Everlasting.' I say wrongly on grounds which cannot be impeached. If in numbers of passages this word confessedly does not and can not mean Endless—a fact, which none but the grossest and most hopelessly ignorant can dispute . . . many scholars who have a good right to be heard deny that it ever necessarily means 'Endless' though it is predicted of endless things. It therefore becomes a clear duty to keep the rendering 'Eternal' which is a neutral word." It should be borne in mind that Dean Farrar first published his views on this interesting subject in 1877. He challenged the traditions of the centuries, and provoked criticism, if not the rage of bigotry in the Anglican Church by his bold declaration. Exactly forty-seven years before, Joseph Smith, in a revelation, which was published to the world a few years afterwards, declared in the name of Diety: "I shall judge every man according to his works, and the deeds which he has done . . . And surely every man must repent or suffer, for I, God, am Endless . . . Nevertheless it is not written that there shall be no end to this torment, but it is written Endless Torment. For, behold . . . I am Endless, and the punishment which is given from my hand is endless punishment, for Endless is my name: wherefore—

"Eternal punishment is God's punishment.

"Endless punishment is God's punishment . . .

"For behold, I God, have suffered these things for all, that they might not suffer if they would repent.—But if they would not repent they must suffer even as I."

In the Pearl of Great Price, which was published in Liverpool, England, in 1851, in a revelation received by Joseph Smith in 1830, which is known as The Book of Moses, the Lord says: "And God spake unto Moses, saying, Behold, I am the Lord God Almighty, and Endless is my name, for I am without beginning of days, or end of years; and is not this endless?"

In a sermon delivered by the Prophet Joseph Smith, October 3, 1841, in which he spoke of salvation for the dead, he said: "There is never a time when the spirit is too old to approach God. All are within reach of pardoning mercy, who have not committed the unpardonable sin, which hath no forgiveness, neither in this world, nor in the world to come. There is a way to release the spirits of the dead; that is by the power and authority of the priesthood—by binding and loosing on earth. This doctrine appears glorious inasmuch as it exhibits the greatness of divine compassion, and benevolence in the extent of the plan of human salvation."

On January 21, 1836, Joseph Smith received the following revelation in the form of a vision:

"All who have died without a knowledge of the gospel, who would have received it had they been permitted to tarry, shall be heirs of the celestial kingdom of God; also all that shall die henceforth without a knowledge of it, who would have received it with all their hearts, shall be heirs of that kingdom, for I, the Lord, will judge all men according to their works, according to the desires of their hearts . . . And I also beheld that all children who die before they arrive at the years of accountability are saved in the celestial kingdom of heaven."

The great trouble with the Catholic and the Protestant

churches, is that they have not wholly understood the plan
of salvation in its fullness as contained in the gospel of Christ.
They recognized the importance of baptism and its absolute
necessity as the "portal of their faith" and consequently required that children, as well as adults, be baptized, that they
might enter the church and kingdom of God. Since this law
was interpreted by them as mandatory, adults and even little
children, dying unbaptized, were supposedly eternally lost.
Neither so-called "original sin" or individual sin could attach
to the innocence of infants so these churches have in the past
suffered the embarrassment of teaching the ungodly doctrine
of the "damnation of infants," and the absolute hopelessness
of the unconverted dead. It was left for the light of a new
Gospel dispensation, inaugurated through the instrumentality
of Joseph Smith, to clear up this question by declaring that little
children have no sin and they have consequently not become
alienate from God, because they were from before the foundations of this earth redeemed by the atonement of Jesus Christ.
The baptism of infants is a futile practice as well as an offense
against the purity of innocent childhood. Their purity and
sinlessness was amply recognized by the Lord when He placed
them upon the pinnacle of holiness in the admonition of His
disciples: "Except ye become as little children ye shall in
nowise enter the kingdom of heaven." Likewise the unbaptized
adults of all time were eternally lost to these churches because
they did not know of the principle of salvation (and baptism) for the dead which would have vindicated the sacrament of baptism as well as the mercy and justice of God.

Between 1840 and 1860 the British Isles were intensely
proselyted by Latter-day Saint missionaries, and the whole
country was literally flooded with our tracts and literature.
Converts to the faith were made by the tens of thousands.
There is no doubt in our minds that these wholesome and
enlightening teachings of the Church shed light and truth upon
this subject in the minds of many who had no sympathy with
the Church. And just as the restored Gospel received by
Joseph Smith gave to mankind again the true idea of God, and
the meaning and power of Priesthood, and the proper mode of

baptism, and defined its precise purpose and the subjects to whom it should be administered; so did the light of the Gospel make known to mankind the fallacy and the unreasonableness of the "hell" and "everlasting" torment envisioned by the Christian world, so did it strike a death blow to the inhuman, and merciless doctrine of "Eternal Damnation" and "Endless Punishment." In like manner the wicked doctrine of damnation of infants was corrected and dispelled by the truth which came to the Church in a revelation received by Joseph Smith in 1830, in which God repudiates the doctrine of Eternal Damnation and the damnation of infants in these words: "And thus did I the Lord God appoint unto man the days of his probation; that by his natural death he might be raised in immortality, and eternal life, even as many as might believe; and they that believe not, unto Eternal Damnation; for they cannot be redeemed from their spiritual fall, because they repent not, for they love darkness rather than light, and their deeds are evil, and they receive their wages of whom they list to obey.

"But behold I say unto you that little children are redeemed from the foundation of the world through mine Only Begotten; Wherefore they cannot sin, for power is not given unto Satan to tempt little children, until they begin to become accountable before me."

(We shall conclude this evening's sermon at this point. We regret that this subject of Salvation for the Dead cannot be completed in one discourse. What we have said tonight, shows conclusively the incompleteness of the gospel as taught by the Churches of Christendom, both Catholic and Protestant, in that the salvation which they offer is altogether inadequate to meet human needs, and is a reflection upon the wisdom, justice, love, mercy, and omnipotence of the Almighty. We shall undertake to show in the sermon of the next two Sunday evenings that the great Anglican Church, in the judgment of a few of its noblest scholars, was utterly lacking in a doctrine that would in any way meet the needs of a salvation that extends hope into the Spirit world. We shall show how some great minds and courageous ministers of that church, under the inspiration of God, declared their belief in a hope beyond the grave. And we shall also see the price they paid, which bordered upon the fate of heretics, in one case at least, for daring to teach their honest convictions on this rational subject called by them the "wider hope.")

III.

IF A MAN DIE IN IMPENITENCE, INDIFFERENCE OR DISOBEDIENCE TO THE GOSPEL, MAY HE BE SAVED?

"And then cometh the redemption of those who are Christ's at his coming; who have received their part in that prison which is prepared for them, that they might receive the gospel and be judged according to men in the flesh." Doc. and Cov. 88:99.

"When Christ comes there will be a class of spirits who will be redeemed from prison, because they will have paid the penalty of transgression and will have accepted the gospel which will have been preached to them in prison."—(L. D. S. Compendium.)

In the sermons of the last two Sunday evenings we spoke of the position of the Catholic Church with respect to the subject of a salvation of the dead. We quoted the authorities of that church on the subject and hope we stated its position fairly when we interpreted the spiritual functions of the church with respect to the departed as entirely limited to the offering of sacrifices and prayers for the dead. The traditions of the church from earliest Christian times down to the present give sanction and approval to this beautiful devotion. In the time of Martin Luther the church, through some of its clerical orders, offered indulgencies for sale which would purchase in some measure purgatorial alleviation to human souls. While Luther pronounced a blessing upon those who spoke against the foolish and impudent language of the preachers of indulgencies he also pronounced a curse upon those who spoke against the indulgencies of the Pope. (See Theses 71, 72). In a letter to Hansen von Rechenberg, 1552, Luther went much farther than the church in this very bold statement: "God forbid that I should limit the time of acquiring faith to the present life! In the depths of the divine mercy there may be opportunity to win it in the future state."

In reforms, mankind always goes—like the pendulum of a clock—from one extreme to another. So it was with respect to the Reformation of the 16th century. The English Church was established by Act of Parliament, with new sermons, ceremonials and liturgies. Protestantism with anti-Catholic passion endeavored to relegate to the scrap heap everything from Rome which to them did not seem essentially Christian. Images, paintings, most of the rituals, and the liturgies were abolished and with this sweeping "reform" went the only vestige of human helpfulness for the departed, namely: prayers for the dead. This left Protestantism, particularly the Church of England, bereft of every semblance of the principle of Christian faith that operates for the salvation of those who have died in ignorance of Christ or without inclination to believe in him. For fully two centuries the great Anglican Church carried on its wonderful ministry with increasing power and intelligence. Not until 1850 to 1870 did the Church of England, through the voice of any of its enlightened ministers, make a public confession that the church seriously lacked important principles of faith that make for a full and complete gospel and an efficient soul-saving church, adequate to all human needs. The first one to be heard on this subject was the late Frederick Denison Maurice. He was born near Lowestoft, in 1805. He was a graduate of Trinity College, Cambridge, and Exeter College, Oxford, graduating from the latter in 1830. In 1840 he was professor of English literature and history and in 1846 occupied the chair of theology at King' College, London. In his lectures before the classes he displayed great learning and remarkable liberality with respect to his religious views, especially upon the subject of the "Wider Hope."

Around him a small group of liberal-minded theologians quickly gathered. They were stoutly resisted by the genuinely orthodox. To illustrate the narrow-mindedness of those days it is said that unbaptized infants were sometimes refused burial in consecrated ground. Prominent among Maurice's supporters were Arthur Penrhyn Stanley, Dean of Westminster, who in a rash moment disregarded all the proprieties of orthodoxy by accepting an invitation from a non-conformist body to unveil a statue erected to the honor and memory of John Bunyan, the author of the immortal allegory "Pilgrim's Progress." With unfettered freedom and Christian tolerance, the dean delivered a delightful tribute to the immortal Baptist tinker who gave the world the exquisite Christian story told in metaphor. The Anglican clergy looked upon this bold disregard of precedent with grave misgivings, and a leading church paper had this to say of the incident: "A statue has been erected to a Non-conformist writer at Bedford. Of course the person invited to unveil it was the inevitable Dean of Westminster. All sorts of persons have statues erected to them in these days. There is a personage, undoubtedly powerful and influential, to whom we quite expect soon to hear that a statue has been erected. (Here followed an elaborate description of the Devil.) When the statue of this personage is finished, we are quite sure that the fittest person to unveil it will be the Dean of Westminster."

It was about this time that Professor Maurice delivered a series of lectures before his class on "The Wider Hope." Most of the members of his class were entirely insensible of the significance of the professor's teachings on this obscure but profound subject. Others eagerly absorbed his liberal views and delighted in the larger aspect of divine love which had been so forcefully taught to them. In this class was the late F. W. Farrar, Dean of Canterbury, who was at that time sixteen years of age. He afterwards confessed that he was thrilled with the love and mercifulness of God as revealed through the teachings of Maurice.

Mr. Plumptre tells us that Professor Maurice had been brought through his studies to commit himself to the love and righteousness of God and in this rhapsody announces his faith in the wider hope: "Immediately these words came into my mind with great power and sweetness. 'In an acceptable time have I heard thee: (Is. XLIX, 8)' And I had then such a view of Christ as made me to cry out, 'Glory, to God in the highest. This is salvation! I know this is salvation!' . . . I saw the ful-

ness, sufficiency, and willingness of Christ to save me and all
men in such a manner as constrained me to venture my soul
into his arms; and if I had had ten thousand souls I could have
trusted them all in his hands. And, O, how I did long, that
every soul of Adam's race might come to know the love of
God in Christ Jesus!"

His views on the subject did not attract very wide attention until he published in 1853, the "Theological Essays" in
which he discussed the Great Freedom, the subject under discussion and this act led to his expulsion from King's College.
Dr. Jeff took up the discussion in a very vigorous manner and
his answer to Professor Maurice formed the indictment which
resulted in his being deposed. Numerous theologians took
sides on the issue. His opponents contended that the Essay
in question contained "opinions and doubt" as to "certain
points of belief" on the "punishment of the wicked" and the
final issue of the "day of judgment" which were of "dangerous tendency, and calculated to unsettle the minds of the
theological students." The continuance of Professor Maurice's
connection with the college would therefore be detrimental to
its usefulness. Even Gladstone concerned himself in what
was going on and made a proposal that Maurice's position be
very carefully considered and that the counsel ascertain
whether or not his views were at variance with the three creeds
and the formularies of the Church of England, but the counsel very promptly rejected Mr. Gladstone's proposal.

Lord Littleton and Bishop Wilberforce had something
to say on the question. One analyzed his offense thus: "That
you teach 'that the revelation of God's love to us in the Gospel
is incompatible with his permitting any of the creatures he has
loved to be consigned to never-ending torment; and that you
therefore do with more or less clearness, revive the old doctrine of the Universalists, that after some unknown period of
torments all such must be restored.' Charles Kingsley was
one of the participants in the great discussion, but all sympathy
for the views of Professor Maurice was of little consequence
in the judgment of the counsel of King's college as it con-

demned his teachings as 'unsettling' and of 'dangerous tendency'."

The result was that in 1853 he was unseated as the professor of theology: "If you want to succeed, conform." He accepted other positions as teacher and finally died on April 1, 1872. A number of dear and devoted friends surrounded him on his death bed. As the end of his life drew near, his kindly comrades in the ministry broke the sad news to him that he would no longer preach the gospel. Though weak and emaciated from years of toil and wasting sickness, he mustered all the energy at his command, and rising in his bed, declared "If I can no longer preach the gospel here, I will preach it in other worlds." (Plumptre Ch. 16, p. 393.)

Poets are prophets. They have the vision of the seer. What the priest of God may declare from the pulpit, the poet may indicate in his inspired verse and the two, as they see and proclaim the truth, are the unrobed servants of God. Tennyson had written in "In Memoriam" these inspired lines which show a larger conception of God's love than was possessed by all the churches of Christendom up to that time:

> "Oh yet we trust that somehow good
> Will be the final goal of ill,
> To pangs of nature, sins of will,
> Defects of doubt, and taints of blood;

> "That nothing walks with aimless feet;
> That not one life shall be destroyed.
> Or cast as rubbish to the void,
> When God hath made the pile complete."

Professor Maurice was Tennyson's godfather and had no doubt kept in close touch with his spiritual son. They viewed these deep and mysterious subjects alike and when dogma did not satisfy they could trust "the larger hope" because they had an abiding faith in divine love. When Tennyson saw his beloved godfather deposed, he sympathetically extended to him an invitation to visit with him:

THE DEGREES OF GLORY

TO THE REV. F. D. MAURICE

Come, when no graver cares employ,
 Godfather, come and see your boy;
Your presence will be sun in winter,
 Making the little one leap for joy.

For, being of that honest few,
 Who give the Fiend himself his due
Should eighty-thousand college-councils
 Thunder "Anathema," friend, at you;

Should all our churchmen foam in spite
 At you, so careful of the right,
Yet one lay-hearth would give you welcome.
 (Take it and come) to the Isle of Wight.
         (January, 1854.)

Dean Frederick W. Farrar in his forceful book, "Eternal Hope," published in 1870, says, "It was from his (Frederick D. Maurice's) books that I learnt the germ of those convictions—once, as I know to my cost, savagely and generally anathematized, now openly professed by multitudes of the clergy—to which I gave expression in my sermons on "Eternal Hope." In his preface he quotes Tennyson and Browning as sources of inspiration and light on this important and penetrating subject. This he quotes from Browning:

> My hope is, a sun shall pierce
> The thickest cloud earth ever stretched;
> That after last, returns the First,
> Through a wide compass round be fetched;
> That what began best, can't end worst,
> Nor what God blessed once, prove accurst."

Farrar states that his lectures which were finally embodied in his book on this subject shook Christianity from center to circumference. He dealt with the following subjects: "What is Heaven"—"Is Life Worth Living"—"Hell, What It Is Not"—"Are There Few That Be Saved"—"Earthly and Future Consequences of Sin." The publication of this book brought upon him much criticism and some commendation, but in order to make his case complete he went to great pains and published in defense of his "Eternal Hope" his "Mercy and Judgment" which was dedicated to Tennyson, in these words:

To
ALFRED TENNYSON, ESQ.,
Poet Laureate,
Etc., Etc.,

Who, among his many high services to
All that is pure in conduct and great in thought
Will also be remembered by Posterity as
The Poet of "The Larger Hope,"
These pages are, by his own kind permission,
Most gratefully and respectfully Dedicated.

In this book, Dean Farrar deals exhaustively with the subject of eternal hope and a salvation for the dead and the preaching of the gospel in the spirit world. He quotes from the fathers, saints, and divines in former ages, and conclusively proves that they were more hopeful and liberal than the ministry of the nineteenth century. He discusses purgatory and the descent of Christ into Hell, prayers for the dead, mitigations, and the milder aspects of future retribution. In one chapter he deals with the subject, "The Second Accretion to Catholic Doctrine—That the Vast Majority of Mankind are Doomed to Endless Torments." He deals with "Jewish Eschatology at the Dawn of the Christian Era," as well as the "Apocryphal Books." "The Targums," and "The Opinions of the Talmudists," and then very exhaustively reviews the "Opinions of the Fathers" from the beginning of Christianity down to the fifteenth and sixteenth centuries. He makes a final appeal to the teachings of the New Testament in support of his doctrine and concludes his book with a Personal Confession of Faith, from which we quote a few of his confessions:

I believe that God willeth all men to be saved.

I believe that God has given to all men the gift of immortality, and that the gifts of God are without repentance.

[130]

I believe that every penitent and pardoned soul will pass from this life into a condition of hope, blessedness, and peace.

I believe that man's destiny stops not at the grave and that many who knew not Christ here will know him there.

I believe that hereafter—whether by means of the "almost sacrament of death" or in other ways unknown to us—God's mercy may reach many who, to all earthly appearance, might seem to us to die in a lost and unregenerate state.

I believe that Christ went and preached to the spirits in prison, and I see reasons to hope that since the gospel was thus once preached "to them that were dead," the offers of God's mercy may in some form be extended to the soul, even after death.

And I believe that to be without God is "hell;" and that in this sense there is a hell beyond the grave; and that for any soul to fall even for a time into this condition, though it be through its own hardened impenitence and resistance of God's grace, is a very awful and terrible prospect; and that in this sense, there may be for some souls an endless hell. But I see reason to hope that through God's mercy, and through the merits of Christ's sacrifice, the great majority of mankind may be delivered from this awful doom. For, according to the Scriptures, though, I know not what its nature will be or how it will be effected.

I believe in the restitution of all things; and

I believe in the coming of that time when,—though in what sense I cannot pretend to explain or to fathom—

God will be All in All.

IV.

As early as 1871 Dr. E. H. Plumptre, Dean of Wells, had manifested his interest in the absorbing subject "The Wider Hope," and on April 30th of that year, he preached a sermon in St. Paul's Cathedral which plainly defined his position on the liberal side of the question. In 1884 he published a volume entitled "The Spirits in Prison" and other studies on "The Life After Death." The dedication of that volume reads thus:

THE VISION

To

The Loved and Honoured Memory
Of
Frederick Denison Maurice,"

and in the preface, he says: "When I wrote in 1871, the two chief epochs in the recent history of the controversies which I then discussed were (1) the expulsion of Mr. F. D. Maurice from King's College in 1859, which made him so to speak, the proto-martyr of the "wider hope;" and (2) the excitement caused by the publication of "Essays and Reviews" in 1860, and the judgment pronounced by the judicial committee of council in the case of Fendall vs. Wilson in 1864. Since that date, Dr. Farrar's sermons, published under the title of Eternal Hope, may fairly be looked on as an "epoch-making book, both in the wide circulation it has attained and the discussion of which it has been the starting point."

Plumptre's book is devoted to an elaborate treatise on the same subject considered in its two predecessors, "Eternal Hope," and "Mercy and Judgment" published nearly ten years earlier by Dean Farrar. It traces with great detail the alignment of the theologians of the English church on the "wider hope" and subjects akin to it from the days of the Reformation down to the date of its publication. Dean Plumptre selected for the title of his book, the text from the epistle of St. Peter where the Apostle states that "Christ went and preached to the spirits in prison." He calls attention on page eighty to one of the apocryphal books to the New Testament, namely: The Gospel of Nicodemus. This composition has no historical value but is unquestionably a production of the very earliest times of the Christian Era. Its authorship is unknown. No claims are made for its genuineness or integrity, but it is very interesting from the fact that as early as the second or third century A. D. there was written a story of very vivid imagination which described in detail the Descent of Christ into Hades. The starting point of the narrative is that two sons of Simeon (see Luke 2), Karinus and Lucius who it appears were among those who had arisen from their graves at the time of the resurrection and had appeared to many. They tell the tale of what they had seen and heard in the world of the dead. They were there with their Father in the thick darkness when suddenly there shone upon them a bright light as of the sun. Adam and the patriarchs and prophets exulted at its coming. Isaiah knew it to be the light that should shine upon those who sat in the region of the shadow of death. Simeon saw that it was the light to lighten the gentiles. John the Baptist, doing there also the work of a forerunner, came to prepare the way and to announce the coming of the Son of God. Seth narrated how Michael the Archangel had told him, as he prayed at the gates of Paradise that one day, after five thousand five hundred years, the Son of God would come to lead His Father Adam into Paradise and to the tree of mercy. Meantime "Hades (here personified as an actor in the drama) and Satan held counsel with each other, and were full of fear. He who had rescued so many of their victims upon earth, who had raised Lazarus from the grave, was now about to invade their kingdom, and to set free all who were shut up in prison, bound with the chain of their sins. And as they spoke, there was a cry like as of thunder: "Lift up your heads, O ye gates, and be ye lifted up, ye everlasting doors, and the King of Glory shall come in."

The Book of Nicodemus herein referred to may be found in the apocrypha to the New Testament, a book easily obtainable.

These three men, Professor Frederick D. Maurice, Dean Frederick W. Farrar, and Dean E. H. Plumptre are the men who were most conspicuous and effective in battling against the creeds and traditions of the English Church as well as all other Christian churches for the "wider hope," or a belief in a salvation for those who had died either in innocent ignorance of Christ or in wilful disobedience of him. The agitation of the question began in the early fifties and reached its climax very quickly in the expulsion of Professor Maurice. The opposition to these views, while entrenched in power at the beginning, made it very uncomfortable for the men who dared to differ with the creeds and challenge the opinions of College cor cils and religious synods. Their following rapidly increased so that by 1877 when Farrar published "Eternal Hope" t ere was no one who dared to seriously question his knowle ge of theology, or the soundness of his position, or the integrity of his faith. The atmosphere was very tranquil when the last exponent of the wider hope, Dean Plumptre came forward with his "Spirits in Prison."

After all, this controversy was little more than an academic discussion of a theological question with the result of liberalizing clerical views and an enlargement, or broadening of Christian sympathy, and the recognition of the larger concept of the love of God for his children. The discussion of the question had a wholesome effect in that it seriously shattered in many minds the false notions and bigoted teachings of many centuries. But all that was done was merely to liberalize to a limited degree the theological views of their time. So far as we can see, their views did not render the slightest practical assistance to the "spirits in prison." Their fetters were not stricken off by this discussion of the English clergy. The gates of hades were not thrown open by the pronouncement of their liberal views, nor was the gospel preached to the spirits in prison by their controversies here on earth. Invaluable from a theological sense as was their heroic defense of their positions, and refreshing and admirable in the highest degree, yet if these accomplishments are to be measured by their actual effectiveness to those over whom all the discussion arose, namely; the departed in the spirit world, nothing that we know of was accomplished. They all conceded the need of such a belief and dared to proclaim it irrespective of the cost to them. They were supported by the New Testament and many early Christian Fathers, as well as some modern ministers, but astonishing as it may seem, the chief opposition which they had to meet was in the established councils of the several churches. Not one of these proponents of the "wider hope," so far as our readings have gone, made a single effectual proposal as to exactly how the spirits in the other world could be redeemed from the darkness of unbelief and the sin of disobedience. They had all read the Apostle Paul's interrogatory to the Corinthians: "Why are they then baptized for the dead?" All of these splendid men subscribed to the ordinance, or sacrament of baptism for the living, but apparently were entirely at a loss to explain the significance of the question propounded by the Apostle Paul concerning the subject. Dean Farrar came as near to the principle as any one, in his studies and pronouncements on the subject. He felt the need of it in order to complete the great saving mission of the Church. He emphasized the indispensability of the doctrine but the great, good man, was at a complete loss as to knowing how to proceed in the matter. In his frank and faithful confessions he says the saving of the dead will be accomplished in some manner "unknown to us." Again, in the same confession he says, "the offer of God's mercy may in some form be extended to the soul even after death." And in further allusions to the nature of the thing to be done for the dead he says "I know not what its nature will be or how it will be effected." And again: "I cannot pretend to explain or to fathom how it will be brought about."

Twenty-five years before this question was raised by Professor Maurice, Joseph Smith had proclaimed a well developed and definite doctrine by which the salvation of the dead was to be effected through the authority in the spirit world where the gospel is continually being preached. These three great and glorious men whose memory we may properly revere, confessedly did not have a full understanding of the gospel.

Listen to the utterances of Joseph Smith upon the subject at a conference of the Church held at Nauvoo, October 2-3, 1841. After explaining the difference between an angel and a disembodied spirit, the Prophet said: "Jesus became a ministering spirit (while his body was lying in the sepulchre) to the spirits in prison, to fulfill an important part of his mission, without which he could not have perfected his work, or entered into his rest. After his resurrection, he appeared as an angel to his disciples." . . . It is no more incredible that God should save the dead, than that he should raise the dead.

THE VISION

"There is never a time when the spirit is too old to approach God. All are within the reach of pardoning mercy, who have not committed the unpardonable sin, which hath no foregiveness, neither in this world, nor in the world to come. There is a way to release the spirits of the dead; that is by the power and authority of the priesthood—by binding and loosing on earth. This doctrine appears glorious, inasmuch as it exhibits the greatness of divine compassion and benevolence in the extent of human salvation.

"This glorious truth is calculated to enlarge the understanding and to sustain the soul under troubles and distresses. For illustration, suppose the case of two men, brothers, equally intelligent, learned, virtuous and lovely, walking in uprightness and in all good conscience, so far as they have been able to discern . . . One dies and is buried, having never heard the gospel of reconciliation; to the other the message of salvation is sent, he hears and embraces it, and is made the heir of eternal life. Shall the one become the partaker of glory and the other be consigned to hopeless perdition? Is there no chance for his escape? Sectarianism answers "None." Such an idea is worse than atheism. The truth shall break down and dash in pieces all such bigoted Pharasaism." Hist. of Ch. vol. 4, p. 425.

The situation may be well illustrated in the experience of Sir William Herschel, the great Anglo-German astronomer. He and his good sister Caroline would spend the nocturnal hours in the study of astronomy, and one night while sweeping the heavens with their hand-made, cardboard telescope, they found the hitherto un-recognized planet Uranus. They knew why to look for it because its existence had been determined by well defined laws known to astronomers but until that night no one had ever regarded this remote planet as a member of our solar system. With the aid of extended vision and an understanding which came from knowledge as to why they should look for this planet, they made the discovery. So with Maurice, Farrar, and Plumptre; they knew that the larger hope was essential to the eternal welfare of the human race and the satisfying of divine love. They felt in their souls that there must be such a thing as a salvation beyond the grave. They knew the direction toward which they should look, but for lack of extended vision and knowledge of the principle engaging their attention, they failed to see this great and glorious principle of the gospel of Jesus Christ, namely; a salvation for the dead through the teaching of the gospel in the spirit world, and the administration of the ordinance of baptism, etc., by the living for the dead.

They saw the necessity for it, but did not see the principle by which it was to be accomplished.

In the earlier vision which was given to Joseph Smith, the angel announced that the spirit of Elijah would be bestowed upon men by which the hearts of the children would be turned to their fathers and the hearts of the fathers would be turned to their children. In other words, the living, after receiving the gospel, would be profoundly concerned over their parents' participating in the blessings of salvation which come through obedience to the gospel. And when the principle of salvation for the dead and baptisms by the living for the dead was revealed to the Church, the hearts of the children were turned intensely toward their fathers who had died before the gospel was restored to the earth. And from evidences of an irresistible character, and in innumerable instances, known to the Latter-day Saints, the hearts of the fathers have manifestly been turned to the children to whom they have steadfastly looked for the performance of the ordinances of the gospel that they might be participators in the salvation provided by Christ. For the purpose of performing this vicarious work for the dead, so far as the dead avail themselves of the opportunities thus afforded, the Latter-day Saints have become a great temple building people for the reason that these sacred ordinances may only be performed in temples erected and dedicated to that holy purpose. Millions of dollars have been spent, millions of days labor have been performed by the Latter-day Saints by which the ordinances of the gospel have been officiated in by the living for the salvation of millions of the dead.

[137]

THE VISION

For the purpose of ascertaining whether or not the hearts of the children have been "turned to their fathers," some years ago, we made inquiry of the largest and oldest genealogical society of New England as to whether or not there has been an appreciable increase in the number of genealogical books and records which have been produced during the last seventy-five years. The very astonishing reply came from the secretary of the society that at the time the society was organized, there were not more than ten inches of books on the shelves of the society. Today, there is a large number of societies with immense libraries some of which contain eleven or twelve thousand printed volumes devoted to genealogies alone. As an illustration of how effectually this work is being done, we recently received from a friend in New York, a volume devoted to the genealogies of our family name which contains detailed information as to names, lineage, marriages, births and deaths of thousands of individuals. And all this information was placed in our hands at a cost of two or three dollars. What impelling motive had moved a well-to-do woman to spend thirty thousand dollars to gather the genealogies of her ancestors back through four centuries, we leave for you to infer. In European countries the incentive for such painstaking and technical work may be to establish right to title of certain heraldic distinctions or interests in large estates, but in America, in hundreds of cases, there are no such incentives. The impelling motive is a heart-felt interest in their fathers who have gone before and this is what the Latter-day Saints believe was predicted by Malachi when he said, speaking for the Lord: "Behold, I will send you Elijah the prophet before the coming of the great and dreadful day of the Lord: And he shall turn the heart of the fathers to the children, and the heart of the children to their fathers, lest I come and smite the earth with a curse."

Concluding we would say that universal Protestantism was entirely devoid of even a semblance of the principle of Salvation of the dead. The Catholic church through the many centuries has sanctioned and observed the beautiful devotion of prayers for the dead. So far as we know it never has declared for prayers for the unconverted but only for the pardon or purging of the faithful of their venial, or trivial sins. The former are the more greatly in need of salvation. Both great religious divisions concede the universal need of baptism for admittance into the Church. Some went so far in the earlier ages as to regard unbaptized children as eternally lost. If the vast majority of mankind is to be saved and if baptism is the divinely ordained media of initiation into the Church of Christ, then why not avail ourselves of the divinely sanctioned ordinance of baptism in the case of the dead? Especially is this question pertinent after the pointed reference of St. Paul to such an ordinance in use by the Church in his day. The universal need of such a principle is very obvious today. Even though the New Testament contains only very meager references to the ordinance yet its need is none-the-less apparent. A Church possessed of the gospel in its fulness would surely have such a principle because the well nigh universal salvation of mankind can be accomplished in no other way known to us. The Church of Jesus Christ of Latter-day Saints is the only Church on the earth that has a knowledge of this principle which throws the doors open to the widest possible salvation of the human race and at the same time observes the sacred ordinance of initiation. This is a very important piece of evidence which goes to prove the Falling Away as well as the Restoration to the earth in its fulness of the Gospel of Jesus Christ.

Yes, the Church of Christ is again upon the earth with a fulness of authority and understanding, and it is equal to all human needs. A Church without this exalted principle of Christian faith falls short of the divine plan and leaves countless millions suffering some such pangs of disappointment as were threateningly promised in the frightful hell of medieval times. May we not thank a kind providence for a hope wider than the most optimistic dreams of man? The Lord has said to us in this, the dawning of a new day: "For behold this is my work and my glory to bring to pass the immortality and the eternal life of man."

THE VISION

"I AM GETTING TIRED AND WOULD LIKE TO GO TO MY REST"

By Joseph the Prophet

"Criticism had already commenced by those near him in authority with regard to his teachings and his doings. And we began now, in a degree, to understand the meaning of what he had so often publicly said, that, should he teach and practice the principle that the Lord had revealed to him, and now requested of him, that those then nearest him in the stand would become his enemies and the first to seek his life; which they soon did, just as he had foretold. And to show you that under conditions then existing that the Prophet really desired no longer to live, and that you may see how my mind was in a degree prepared for after results I will briefly relate an incident that occurred at his last visit to us at Ramus.

"After he had at evening preached with great animation to a large congregation, and had blessed nineteen children, he turned and said to me, 'Benjamin, I am tired, let us go home,' which, only a block distant, we soon reached, and entering we found a warm fire with a large chair in front, and my wife sitting near with her oldest upon her lap, and approaching I said: 'Now Melissa, see what we have lost by not going to meeting, Brother Joseph has blessed all the children in the place but ours, and it is left out in the cold.' But the Prophet at once said, 'You shall lose nothing,' and he proceeded to bless our first-born, and then, with a deep drawn breath as a sign of weariness, he sank down heavily in his chair, and said, 'Oh! I do get so tired and weary that at times I almost yearn for my rest,' and then proceeded to briefly recount to us some of the most stirring events of his life's labors, sufferings and sacrifices, and then he said, 'I am getting tired and would like to go to my rest.' His words and tone thrilled and shocked me, and like an arrow, pierced my hopes that he would long remain with us, and I said, as with a heart full of tears: 'O Joseph, what could we, as a people, do without you and what would become of the great latter-day work if you should leave us?' He saw and was touched by my emotions, and in reply he said, 'Benjamin, I would not be far away from you, and if on the other side of the veil, I would still be working with you, and with a power greatly increased, to roll on this kingdom.' Such was the tone, earnestness and pathos of his words to me then, that they cannot be fully recalled but with emotion."

(Excerpt from letter from Patriarch Benjamin F. Johnson to George S. Gibbs of Salt Lake City)

ह❧

THE GRATITUDE THAT WILL BE MANIFESTED BY THOSE FOR WHOM VICARIOUS TEMPLE WORK WILL BE PERFORMED

By JOSEPH THE PROPHET

"Concerning the Prophet's preaching, I have heard father say that although he was a powerful speaker and could hold his audience spellbound, he seemed to feel an inability to make them really comprehend what he taught them, and showed great anxiety to do so. Here are a few points that father heard him teach:

'It would have been contrary to the oath and covenant that belong to the Priesthood for Lot and his family to have been destroyed with Gomorrah, so the Lord sent an angel to get them out, as Lot held the Priesthood.'

"Concerning the work for the dead, he said that in the resurrection those who had been worked for would fall at the feet of those who had done their work, kiss their feet, embrace their knees and manifest the most exquisite gratitude. We do not comprehend what a blessing to them these ordinances are. Father was so impressed with these teachings that he spent the last ten years of his life working in Temples, and has transmitted the same inclination to his posterity. We have worked for over 5,000 of our dead and have as many more to do."

(The above was dictated to the Compiler of this work by Horace Cummings, who was formerly Superintendent of Church Schools)

DO THE DEPARTED APPRECIATE VICARIOUS WORK PERFORMED FOR THEM?

(A vision given to Horatio Pickett, March 19, 1914)

"While working here in the St. George Temple, I often thought of the great expense and the time and labor necessary to support the Temple, and to perform the necessary ordinances therein for the salvation of the dead, and the question often arose in my mind: Do they (the dead) know what is being done for them and do they appreciate the sacrifice that is being made by their brethren and sisters in the Temples for their benefit.

"I often asked the Lord to give me sufficient of His Spirit that I might have a better understanding of the Temple work than I had. One day while at the font confirming, when a large list of women were being baptized for, the thought again came into my mind: Do those people for whom this work is being done, know that it is being done for them, and, if they do, do they appreciate it? While this thought was running through my mind I happened to turn my eyes toward the south-east corner of the font room and there I saw a large group of women. The whole south-east part of the room was filled; they seemed to be standing a foot or more above the floor and were all intently watching the baptizing that was being done; and as the recorder called a name, one of them—a rather tall, very slim woman, apparently about 35 years of age, gave a sudden start and looked at the recorder. Then her eyes turned to the couple in the water, closely watching the baptism; then her eyes followed the sister that was being baptized as she came up out of the water and was confirmed, and when the ordinance was completed the happy, joyous expression that spread over her countenance was lovely to behold.

"The next one called seemed to be a younger woman, a little below the average height. She was of a nervous, emotional nature, could not keep still, seemed as though she wanted to jump into the water herself, and when the ordinance was finished she seemed to be overflowing with joy, turning from one to another of her companions as though she was telling them how happy she was.

"The third was a large muscular-looking woman, not fleshy but bony, masculine build, very high forehead and intelligent countenance, hair streaked with gray and combed like elderly ladies used to wear their hair when I was a lad. She seemed to be of a more quiet, stoical nature than the others; no outward demonstration of what her feelings may have been, but there was a look in her eyes that seemed to say that she appreciated what was being done fully as much as the others did, and when the ceremony was finished she nodded her head slightly and moved her lips as though she might have said, 'Amen'.

"Just as the work for her was finished there was a noise in President Cannon's office as though a book or something might have fallen to the floor which caused me to turn my eyes in that direction, and though I turned back instantly, the vision had faded and gone and with it also had gone all doubt and queries that may have been in mind on the subject. I was satisfied, and am still satisfied that our friends behind the veil know and realize what is being done for them and are anxiously waiting for their time to come.

"I do not think it would be possible for any person to look into the faces of those women as I did and see the earnestness with which they were watching the proceedings, and the joy and happiness that shone in their faces as their names were called and the work done for them, and not feel as I do. This was not a night vision nor a dream but was about three o'clock on a bright, sunny afternoon while I was standing at the font assisting in the ordinances thereof."

Contributed by Martin L. McAllister of St. George, Utah

ॐ

TRANSLATIONS OF I CORINTHIANS 15:29

King James' Translation: "Else what shall they do which are baptized for the dead, if the dead rise not at all? Why are they then baptized for the dead?"

Revised Version: "Else what shall they do which are baptized for the dead? if the dead are not raised at all, why are they baptized for them?"

American Standard: "Else what shall they do that are baptized for the dead? If the dead are not raised at all, why are they then baptized for them?"

Moffatt's New Testament (1913): "Otherwise, if there is no such thing as a resurrection, what is the meaning of people getting baptized on behalf of their dead? If dead men do not rise at all, why do people get baptized on their behalf, yea, and why am I in danger every hour?"

Wescott & *Horts*: (Rev. ed. Revell & Co. in Twentieth Century New Testament): "Again, what good will they be doing who are baptized in behalf of the dead? If it is true, that the dead do not rise, why are people baptized on their behalf?"

Wycliff (Ed. of 1380 as revised by Purvey in 1388): "Ellis what schulen thei do, that ben baptisid for deed men, if in no wise deed men risen agen? whereto ben thei baptisid for hem?"

Wilson Emphatic Diaglott (literal word for word with Greek): "Otherwise what shall they do, those being dipped on behalf of the dead ones, if at all dead ones not are raised up? why and are they dipped on behalf of them?"

Sharpe's Greek New Testament: "Else what shall they do who are being baptized over the dead, if the dead are not raised at all? why are they then being baptized over them?"

Goodspeed (*New Testament, An American Translation*): "Otherwise what do people mean by having themselves baptized on behalf of their dead? If the dead do not rise at all, why do they have themselves baptized on their behalf?"

Conybeare & *Howson* (In Life & Epistles of St. Paul): "Again, what will become of those who cause themselves to be baptized for the dead, if the dead never rise again? Why do they then submit to baptism for the dead?"

Quintus Septimus Florens Terullianus (In De. Res. c. 48): "Why are they then baptized for the dead unless the bodies rise again which are thus baptized?"

Douay (*Catholic*) *Bible*: "Otherwise what shall they do that are baptized for the dead if the dead rise not again at all? Why are they then baptized for them?"

Wilson Emphatic Diaglott (literal translation): "Otherwise what will those do who are being immersed on behalf of the dead? If the dead are not raised at all, why then are they immersed on their behalf?"

Syriac Versions "Otherwise what shall they do who are baptized for the dead if the dead rise not? Why are they baptized for the dead?" (Murdock's Translation of the Syriac New Testament.)

ও

ORIGIN AND DESTINY OF WOMAN

By President John Taylor

"The Latter-day Saints have often been ridiculed on account of their belief in the pre-existence of spirits, and for marrying for time and all eternity, both being Bible doctrines. We have often been requested to give our views in relation to these principles, but considered the things of the kingdom belonged to the children of the kingdom, therefore not meet to give them to those without. But being very politely requested by a lady a few days since (a member of the Church) to answer the following questions, we could not consistently refuse, viz.:

" 'Where did I come from? What am I doing here? Whither am I going? And what is my destiny after having obeyed the truth, if faithful to the end?'

"For her benefit and all others concerned, we will endeavor to answer the questions in brief, as we understand them. The reason will be apparent for our belief in the pre-existence of spirits, and in marrying for time and all eternity.

"Lady, whence comest thou? Thine origin? What art thou doing here? Whither art thou going, and what is thy destiny? Declare unto me if thou hast understanding. Knowest thou not that thou art a spark of Deity, struck from the fire of His eternal blaze, and brought forth in the midst of eternal burning?

"Knowest thou not that eternities ago thy spirit, pure and holy, dwelt in thy Heavenly Father's bosom, and in His presence, and with thy mother, one of the queens of heaven, surrounded by thy brother and sister spirits in the spirit world, among the Gods? That as thy spirit beheld the scenes transpiring there, and thou grewest in intelligence, thou sawest worlds upon worlds organized and peopled with thy kindred spirits who took upon them tabernacles, died, were resurrected, and received their exaltation on the redeemed worlds they once dwelt upon. Thou being willing and anxious to imitate them, waiting and desirous to obtain a body, a resurrection and exaltation also, and having obtained permission, madest a covenant with one of thy kindred spirits to be thy guardian angel while in mortality, also with two others, male and female spirits, that thou wouldst come and take a tabernacle through their lineage, and become one of their offspring. You also chose a kindred spirit whom you loved in the spirit world (and who had permission to come to this planet and take a tabernacle), to be your head, stay, husband and protector on the earth and to exalt you in eternal worlds. All these were arranged, likewise the spirits that should tabernacle through your lineage. Thou longed, thou sighed and thou prayed to thy Father in heaven for the time to arrive when thou couldst come to this earth, which had fled and fallen from where it was first organized, near the planet Kolob. Leaving thy father and mother's bosom and all thy kindred spirits thou camest to earth, took a tabernacle, and imitated the deeds of those who had been exalted before you.

"At length the time arrived, and thou heard the voice of thy Father saying, go daughter to yonder lower world, and take upon thee a tabernacle, and work out thy probation with fear and trembling and rise to exaltation. But daughter, remember you go on this condition, that is, you are to forget all things you ever saw, or knew to be transacted in the spirit world; you are not to know or remember anything concerning the same that you have beheld transpire here; but you must

[146]

go and become one of the most helpless of all beings that I have created, while in your infancy, subject to sickness, pain, tears, mourning, sorrow and death. But when truth shall touch the cords of your heart they will vibrate; then intelligence shall illuminate your mind, and shed its lustre in your soul, and you shall begin to understand the things you once knew, but which had gone from you; you shall then begin to understand and know the object of your creation. Daughter, go, and be faithful as thou hast been in thy first estate.

"Thy spirit, filled with joy and thanksgiving, rejoiced in thy Father, and rendered praise to His holy name, and the spirit world resounded in anthems of praise to the Father of spirits. Thou bade father, mother and all farewell, and along with thy guardian angel, thou came on this terraqueous globe. The spirits thou hadst chosen to come and tabernacle through their lineage, and your head having left the spirit world some years previous, thou came a spirit pure and holy. Thou hast obeyed the truth, and thy guardian angel ministers unto thee and watches over thee. Thou hast chosen him you loved in the spirit world to be thy companion. Now crowns, thrones, exaltations and dominions are in reserve for thee in the eternal worlds, and the way is opened for thee to return back into the presence of thy Heavenly Father, if thou wilt only abide by and walk in a celestial law, fulfill the designs of thy Creator and hold out to the end that when mortality is laid in the tomb, you may go down to your grave in peace, arise in glory, and receive your everlasting reward in the resurrection of the just, along with thy head and husband. Thou wilt be permitted to pass by the Gods and angels who guard the gates, and onward, upward to thy exaltation in a celestial world among the Gods. To be a priestess queen upon thy Heavenly Father's throne, and a glory to thy husband and offspring, to bear the souls of men, to people other worlds (as thou didst bear their tabernacles in mortality) while eternity goes and eternity comes; and if you will receive it, lady, this is eternal life. And herein is the saying of the Apostle Paul fulfilled, 'That the man is not without the woman, neither is the woman without the man in the Lord.' 'That the man is the head of the woman, and the glory of the man is the woman.' Hence, thine origin, the object of thy ultimate destiny. If faithful, lady, the cup is within thy reach; drink then the heavenly draught and live."

"The Mormon," August 29, 1857, New York City.

ॐ

"OH, YE SAINTS OF LATTER DAYS, DO NOT FORGET THE HIGH DESTINY THAT AWAITS YOU"

"I feel as though the day has come when every Elder and every Latter-day Saint ought to stop and consider the position he is in and the covenants he has entered into. Is there anything on the face of the earth that will pay you to depart from the Oracles of God and from the gospel of Christ? Is there anything that will pay you to lose the principles of salvation, to lose a part of the first resurrection with the privilege of standing in the morning of the resurrection clothed with glory, immortality and eternal life at the head of your father's house? No, there is nothing. I feel sorry many time when I see men who have the Priesthood forget almost that they have any interest in the work of God."

(Pres. Wilford Woodruff, Gen. Con. Report, Apr. 10, 1898, p. 90.)

"Oh, ye Saints of the Latter Days, do not forget the high destiny that awaits you. An eternity is before you, which has no end; a boundless space surrounds you, filled with an infinitude of worlds. The kingdoms, principalities, and heavenly powers that fill all the vast expanse are yours; the heights and depths, the lengths and breadths, the riches and honors, the wisdom and excellency, the knowledge and power, the glory of all things, and the fullness of all things, are yours for ever and ever. Blessed is he that overcometh, for he shall inherit all things."

Orson Pratt, in "The Seer," page 300.

THE MISERY OF FALLEN ANGELS

By Elder Orson Pratt

"If we should inquire what constitutes the misery of the fallen angels, the answer would be, they are destitute of love; they have ceased to love God; they have ceased to have pure love one towards another; they have ceased to love that which is good. Hatred, malice, revenge, and every evil passion have usurped the place of love; and unhappiness, wretchedness, and misery are the results. Where there is no love, there will be no desire to promote the welfare of others. Instead of desiring that others may be happy, each desires to make all others miserable like himself; each seeks to gratify that hellish disposition against the Almighty which arises from his extreme hatred of that which is good. For the want of love the torment of each is complete. All the wicked who are entirely overcome by these malicious spirits will have the heavenly principle of love wholly eradicated from their minds, and they will become angels to these infernal fiends, being captivated by them, and compelled to act as they act. They cannot extricate themselves from their power, nor ward off the fiery darts of their malicious tormentors. Such will be the condition of all beings who entirely withdraw themselves from the love of God. As love decreases, wickedness, hatred, and misery increase; and the more wicked individuals or nations become, the less capable are they of loving others and making them happy; and vice versa, the more righteous a people become, the more they are qualified for loving others and rendering them happy. A wicked man can have but little love for his wife, while a righteous man, being filled with the love of God, is sure to manifest this heavenly attribute in every thought and feeling of his heart, and in every word and deed. Love, joy, and innocence will radiate from his very countenance, and be expressed in every look. This will beget confidence in the wife of his bosom, and she will love him in return; for love begets love; happiness imparts happiness; and these heaven-born emotions will continue to increase more and more, until they are perfected and glorified in all the fulness of eternal love itself.

THE VISION

"Could wicked and malicious beings, who have eradicated every feeling of love from their bosoms, be permitted to propagate their species, the offspring would partake of all the evil, wicked, and malicious nature of their parents. However pure the spirits might be, when permitted to enter such degraded tabernacles, yet, being extremely susceptible to influences, they would speedily partake of all the evil nature which characterized the spirits of the father and mother; thus they would soon become devils incarnated in flesh and bones. Such would be the dreadful consequences of offspring, brought into existence by parents destitute of the principles of love, like the fallen angels. The same consequences, to a certain degree, would result from the multiplication of wicked parents. In proportion as the pure love of God is eradicated from their hearts, the unholy passions take the place thereof, and the offspring partake of these unlovely principles which are engendered in the nature and constitution of the infant tabernacle, and begin to act upon the pure spirit that takes up its abode therein, forming, modifying, and bending, in a great measure, its inclinations, until, by the time that it grows up to know good from evil, it becomes prepared to plunge headlong into all the vices of its ungodly parents; thus the parents, for the want of that holy and pure affection which exists in the bosom of the righteous, not only destroy their own happiness, but impress their own degraded and unlovely passions upon the constitution of their offspring. It is for this reason that God will not permit the fallen angels to multiply: it is for this reason that God has ordained marriages for the righteous only: it is for this reason that God will put a final stop to the multiplication of the wicked after this life.

—*The Seer, pp.* 156-7.

ह∾

IN THE LINEAGE OF THE GODS

By President Lorenzo Snow
Excerpts from article entitled: "Devotion to a Divine Inspiration"
by LeRoi C. Snow

"In May, 1836, after a blessing meeting, to which he had been invited, in the Kirtland Temple, the Patriarch, Father

Joseph Smith, said to Lorenzo Snow: 'You will soon be convinced of the truth of the latter-day work, and be baptized, and you will become as great as you can possibly wish—even as great as God, and you cannot wish to be greater.'

"What a remarkable promise! It astonished the young man and awakened thoughts in his mind of which he had never before dreamed. Two weeks later, in June, 1836, at the age of twenty-two, he was baptized by Apostle John Boynton.

* * * "In the spring of 1840, just before leaving on his first mission to England, Lorenzo Snow spent an evening in the home of his friend, Elder H. G. Sherwood, in Nauvoo. Elder Sherwood was endeavoring to explain the parable of the Savior about the husbandman who sent forth servants at different hours of the day to labor in the vineyard. While thus engaged in thought this most important event occurred, as told by President Snow himself:

'While attentively listening to his (Elder Sherwood's) explanation, the Spirit of the Lord rested mightily upon me—the eyes of my understanding were opened, and I saw as clear as the sun at noonday, with wonder and astonishment, the pathway of God and man. I formed the following couplet which expresses the revelation, as it was shown to me, and explains Father Smith's dark saying to me at a blessing meeting in the Kirtland temple, prior to my baptism, as previously mentioned in my first interview with the Patriarch:

As man now is, God once was;
As God now is, man may be.

I felt this to be a sacred communication which I related to no one except my sister Eliza, until I reached England, when in a confidential, private conversation with President Brigham Young, in Manchester, I related to him this extraordinary manifestation.'

"Soon after his return from England, in January, 1843, Lorenzo Snow related to the Prophet Joseph Smith his experience in Elder Sherwood's home. This was in a confidential interview in Nauvoo. The Prophet's reply was: 'Brother Snow, that is true gospel doctrine, and it is a revelation from God to you.'

"Let us understand clearly that while Lorenzo Snow, through a revelation from God, was the author of the above couplet expression, the Lord had revealed this great truth to the Prophet and to Father Smith, long before it was made known to Lorenzo Snow. In fact, it was the remarkable promise given to him in the Kirtland temple, in 1836, by the Patriarch that first awakened the thought in his mind, and its expression in the frequently quoted couplet was not revealed to President Snow until the spring of 1840. We cannot emphasize the fact too strongly that this revealed truth impressed Lorenzo Snow more than perhaps all else; it sank so deeply into his soul that it became the inspiration of his life and gave him his broad vision of his own great future and the mighty mission and work of the Church.

"Four years after this revelation to Lorenzo Snow, and more than a year after he related it to Joseph Smith, the Prophet himself expressed the same idea in a public sermon. This was during the General Conference, Sunday afternoon, April 7, 1844. In referring to the death, a short time before, of Elder King Follet, the Prophet preached a general funeral sermon. This was one of his last sermons, as the martyrdom occurred less than three months later. This sermon was first published, in part, about six weeks after the martyrdom, in the August 15, 1844, issue of the *Times and Seasons,* and seventeen years afterward, in 1861, it appeared in Vol. 23 of the Millennial Star. It was also printed in the January number of the *Improvement Era,* in 1909, with explanatory footnotes by Elder B. H. Roberts."

Improvement Era, Vol. 22, No. 8—June, 1919.

ช๖

MARRYING OUTSIDE THE CHURCH

(See also article by Orson Pratt on page 91)

By President Brigham Young

"Be careful, O ye mothers in Israel, and do not teach your daughters in future, as many of them have been taught, to marry out of Israel. Woe to you who do it; you will lose your crowns as sure as God lives."

J-D. 12:304.

By Parley P. Pratt

"I now wish to say a few words on the subject of matrimony and also on the subject of raising and educating children.

"Who that has had one glimpse of the order of the celestial family and of the eternal connections and relationships which should be formed here in order to be enjoyed there; who that has felt one thrill of the energy and power of eternal life and love which flows from the divine spirit of revelation, can ever be contented with the corrupt pleasures of a moment which arise from the unlawful connections and desires? Or what Saint who has any degree of faith in the power of the resurrection and of eternal life, can be contented to throw themselves away by matrimonial connections with sectarians or other worldlings who are so blind that they can never secure an eternal union by the authority of the Holy Priesthood which has power to bind that which shall be bound in heaven? By such a union, or by corrupt, unlawful and unvirtuous connections and indulgences they not only lose their own celestial crown and throne, but also plunge their children into ruin and darkness, which will probably cause them to neglect so great a salvation for the sake of the love and the praise of the world and the traditions of men.

"O my friends—my brethren and sisters, and especially the younger class of our community: I beseech you in the fear and love of God and entreat you in view of eternal glory and exaltation in His kingdom, to deny yourselves all the corrupt and abominable practices and desires of the world and the flesh, and seek to be pure and virtuous in all your ways and thoughts, and not only so, but make no matrimonial connections or engagements till you have asked counsel of the Spirit of God in humble prayer before Him; till you know and understand the principles of eternal life and union sufficiently to act wisely and prudently, and in that way that will eventually secure yourself and companion and your children in the great family circle of the celestial organization.

[153]

THE VISION

"I would now say to parents that their own salvation, as well as that of their children, depends to a certain extent on the bringing up of their children, and educating them in the truth, that their traditions and early impressions may be correct. No parent who continues to neglect this after they themselves have come to the knowledge of the truth, can be saved in the celestial kingdom.

From "The Prophet," published in New York City, 1845.

By President Joseph F. Smith

"I would rather go myself to the grave than to be associated with a wife outside of the bonds of the new and everlasting covenant. Now, I hold it just so sacred; but some members of the Church do not so regard the matter. Some people feel that it does not make very much difference whether a girl marries a man in the Church, full of the faith of the gospel, or an unbeliever. Some of our young people have married outside the Church, but very few of those who have done it have failed to come to grief. I would like to see Latter-day Saint women marry Latter-day Saint men, and Latter-day Saint men marry Latter-day Saint women; and let Methodists marry Methodists, Catholics marry Catholics, and Presbyterians marry Presbyterians, and so on to the limit. Let them keep within the pale of their own faith and church, and marry and inter-marry there, and let the Latter-day Saints do the same thing in their Church; then we will see who comes out best in the end."

October Conference Report, 1909, pp. 5-6.

ह्श्

ETERNITY SKETCHED IN A VISION FROM GOD
—A POEM

The following poem was first published in the *Times and Seasons,* and was later published in the *Millennial Star* (August, 1843, Vol. IV, No. 4). It is again reprinted in this book— THE VISION—together with a portion of the foreword that accompanied its publication in the *Millennial Star,* as follows:

THE DEGREES OF GLORY

"The following very curious poetic composition is at once both novel and interesting, for while the common landmarks of modern poetry are entirely disregarded, there is something so dignified and exalted conveyed in the ideas of this production, that it cannot fail to strike the attention of every superficial observer.

"Concerning the style of the poetry, there seems to be a native simplicity—a brilliance of thought—and an originality in the composition, that can only be equalled in the oracles of truth and by those who profess the same spirit; and when the muse of those ancient poets was fired by the spirit of God, and they spake as they were moved by the Holy Ghost, there was a richness, a dignity, and a brilliancy of ideas, and an exuberance of thought that ran through all their productions, as in the fascinating beauties of poesy they rolled forth the words of eternal life, with all their richness, and dignity, and glory, while at the same time they paid little or no attention to the rules of poetic composition. Let the curtains of heaven be withdrawn, and the purposes and glories of the eternal world burst upon his view, and the dry forms and simple jingling of rhyme alone, will be very dry and insipid to the enlarged and enlightened understanding of the man of God."

FROM W. W. PHELPS TO JOSEPH SMITH, THE PROPHET.

VADE MECUM.

Go with me, will you go to the Saints that have died—
To the next better world where the righteous reside?
Where the angels and spirits in harmony be,
In the joys of a vast paradise?—Go with me.

> Go with me where the truth and the virtues prevail;
> Where the union is one, and the years never fail;
> Not a heart can conceive, nor a nat'ral eye see
> What the Lord has prepar'd for the just.—Go with me.

Go with me where there's no destruction or war;
Neither tyrants or sland'rers, nor nations ajar;
Where the system is perfect, and happiness free,
And the life is eternal with God.—Go with me.

> Go with me, will you go to the mansions above,
> Where the bliss, and the knowledge, the light, and the love,
> And the glory of God do eternally be?
> Death, the wages of sin, is not there.—Go with me.

Nauvoo, January, 1843.

[155]

THE VISION

FROM JOSEPH SMITH TO W. W. PHELPS, ESQ.

A VISION

I will go, I will go, to the home of the Saints,
    Where the virtue's the value, and life the reward;
But before I return to my former estate,
    I must fulfil the mission I had from the Lord.

        Wherefore, hear O ye heavens, and give ear O ye earth,
           And rejoice, ye inhabitants, truly again;
        For the Lord he is God, and his life never ends,
           And besides him there ne'er was a Savior of men.

His ways are a wonder, his wisdom is great;
    The extent of his doings there's none can unveil;
His purposes fail not; from age unto age
    He still is the same, and his years never fail.

        His throne is the heavens—his life-time is all
           Of eternity *now,* and eternity *then;*
        His union is power, and none stays his hand,
           The Alpha, Omega, for ever. Amen.

For thus saith the Lord, in the spirit of truth,
    I am merciful, gracious, and good unto those
That fear me, and live for the life that's to come:
    My delight is to honour the Saints with repose,

        That serve me in righteousness true to the end;
           Eternal's their glory and great their reward.
        I'll surely reveal all my myst'ries to them—
           The great hidden myst'ries in my kingdom stor'd;

From the council in Kolob, to time on the earth,
    And for ages to come unto them I will show
My pleasure and will, what the kingdom will do:
    Eternity's wonders they truly shall know.

        Great things of the future I'll show unto them,
           Yea, things of the vast generations to rise;
        For their wisdom and glory shall be very great,
           And their pure understanding extend to the skies.

And before them the wisdom of wise men shall cease,
    And the nice understanding of prudent ones fail!
For the light of my spirit shall light mine elect,
    And the truth is so mighty 'twill ever prevail.

THE DEGREES OF GLORY

And the secrets and plans of my will I'll reveal,
    The sanctifi'd pleasures when earth is renew'd;
What the eye hath not seen, nor the ear hath yet heard,
    Nor the heart of the natural man ever view'd.

I, Joseph, the phophet, in spirit beheld,
    And the eyes of the inner man truly did see
Eternity sketch'd in a vision from God,
    Of what was, and now is, and yet is to be.

    Those things which the Father ordained of old,
        Before the world was or a system had run;
    Through Jesus, the Maker and Savior of all—
        The only begotten (Messiah) his son.

Of whom I bear record, as all prophets have,
    And the record I bear is the fulness—yea, even
The truth of the gospel of Jesus—*the Christ,*
    With whom I convers'd in the vision of heav'n.

    For while in the act of translating his word,
        Which the Lord in his grace had appointed to me,
    I came to the gospel recorded by John,
        Chapter fifth, and the twenty-ninth verse which you'll see.

Which was given as follows. Speaking of the resurrection of the dead, concerning those who shall hear the voice of the Son of Man:—

"And shall come forth; they who have done good in the resurrection of the just, and they who have done evil in the resurrection of the unjust."

I marvell'd at these resurrections, indeed,
    For it came unto me by the spirit direct:
And while I did meditate what it all meant,
    The Lord touch'd the eyes of my own intellect.

    Hosanna, for ever! They open'd anon,
        And the glory of God shone around where I was;
    And there was the Son at the Father's right hand,
        In a fulness of glory and holy applause.

I beheld round the throne holy angels and hosts,
    And sanctified beings from worlds that have been,
In holiness worshipping God and the Lamb,
    For ever and ever. Amen and amen.

THE VISION

And now after all of the proofs made of him,
By witnesses truly, by whom he was known,
This is mine, last of all, that he lives; yea, he lives!
And sits at the right hand of God on his throne.

And I heard a great voice bearing record from heav'n,
He's the Saviour and only begotten of God;
By him, of him, and through him, the worlds were all made,
Even all that career in the heavens so broad.

Whose inhabitants, too, from the first to the last,
Are sav'd by the very same Saviour of ours;
And, of course, are begotten God's daughters and sons
By the very same truths and the very same powers.

And I saw and bear record of warfare in heaven;
For an angel of light, in authority great,
Rebell'd against Jesus and sought for his power,
But was thrust down to woe from his glorified state.

And the heavens all wept, and the tears dropp'd like dew.
That Lucifer, son of the morning, had fell!
Yea, is fallen! is fallen and become, oh alas!
The son of perdition, the devil of hell!

And while I was yet in the spirit of truth,
The commandment was—"Write ye the vision all out,
For Satan, old serpent, the devil's for war,
And yet will encompass the Saints round about."

And I saw, too, the suff'ring and misery of those
(Overcome by the devil, in warfare and fight,)
In hell-fire and vengeance—the doom of the damn'd;
For the Lord said the vision is further, so write:

For thus saith the Lord, now concerning all those,
Who know of my power and partake of the same;
And suffer themselves that they be overcome
By the power of Satan, despising my name—

Defying my power, and denying the truth:
They are they of the world, or of men most forlorn
The sons of perdition, of whom, ah! I say,
'Twere better for them had they never been born

THE DEGREES OF GLORY

They're the vessels of wrath, and dishonour to God,
  Doom'd to suffer his wrath in the regions of woe,
Through all the long night of eternity's round,
  With the devil and all of his angels below.

    Of whom it is said no forgiveness is found,
      In this world, alas! nor the world that's to come
    For they have deny'd the spirit of God,
      After having receiv'd it, and mis'ry's their doom.

And denying the only begotten of God,
  And crucify him to themselves, as they do,
And openly put him to shame in their flesh,
  By gospel they cannot repentence renew.

    They are they who go to the great lake of fire,
      Which burneth with brimstane, yet never consumes,
    And dwell with the devil, and angels of his,
      While eternity goes and eternity comes.

They are they who must groan through the great second death,
  And are not redeemed in the time of the Lord;
While all the rest are, through the triumph of Christ,
  Made partakers of grace, by the power of his word.

    The myst'ry of godliness truly is great;
      The past, and the present, and what is to be;
    And this is the gospel—glad tidings to all,
      Which the voice from the heavens bore record to me

That he came to the world in the middle of time,
  To lay down his life for his friends and his foes,
And bear away sin as a mission of love,
  And sanctify earth for a blessed repose.

    'Tis decreed that he'll save all the work of his hands,
      And sanctify them by his own precious blood;
    And purify earth for the Sabbath of rest,
      By the agent of fire as it was by the flood.

The Saviour will save all his Father did give,
  Even all that he gave in the regions abroad,
Save the sons of perdition—they are lost, ever lost!
  And can never return to the presence of God.

THE VISION

They are they who must reign with the devil in hell,
    In eternity now, and eternity then!
Where the worm dieth not, and the fire is not quench'd,
    And the punishment still is eternal. Amen.

And which is the torment apostates receive,
    But the end or the place where the torment began,
Save to them who are made to partake of the same,
    Was never, nor will be revealed unto man.

    Yet God, by a vision, shows a glimpse of their fate,
        And straightway he closes the scene that was shown;
    So the width, or the depth, or the misery thereof,
        Save to those that partake, is forever unknown.

And while I was pondering, the vision was closed,
    And the voice said to me, write the vision; for, lo!
'Tis the end of the scene of the sufferings of those,
    Who remain filthy still in their anguish and woe.

    And again I bear record of heavenly things,
        Where virtue's the value above all that is priz'd,
    Of the truth of the gospel concerning the just,
        That rise in the first resurrection of Christ.

Who receiv'd, and believ'd, and repented likewise,
    And then were baptiz'd as a man always was,
Who ask'd and receiv'd a remission of sin,
    And honoured the kingdom by keeping its laws.

    Being buried in water, as Jesus had been,
        And keeping the whole of his holy commands,
    They received the gift of the spirit of truth,
        By the ordinance truly of laying on hands.

For these overcome, by their faith and their works,
    Being tried in their life-time, as purified gold,
And seal'd by the spirit of promise to life,
    By men called of God, as was Aaron of old.

    They are they, of the church of the first-born of God,
        And unto whose hands he committeth all things;
    For they hold the keys of the kingdom of heav'n,
        And reign with the Saviour, as priests and as kings.

THE DEGREES OF GLORY

They're priests of the order of Melchizedek,
 Like Jesus (from whom is this highest reward),
Receiving a fulness of glory and light;
 As written—they're Gods even sons of the Lord.

  So all things are theirs; yea, of life or of death;
   Yea, whether things now, or to come, all are theirs,
  And they are the Saviour's, and he is the Lord's,
   Having overcome all, as eternity's heirs.

'Tis wisdom that man never glory in man,
 But give God the glory for all that he hath;
For the righteous will walk in the presence of God,
 While the wicked are trod under foot in his wrath.

  Yea, the righteous shall dwell in the presence of God,
   And of Jesus, forever, from earth's second birth—
  For when he comes down in the splendour of heav'n,
   All those he'll bring with him to reign on the earth.

These are they that arise in their bodies of flesh,
 When the trump of the first resurrection shall sound;
These are they that come up to Mount Zion, in life,
 Where the blessings and gifts of the spirit abound.

  These are they that have come to the heavenly place;
   To the numberless courses of angels above:
  To the city of God, e'en the holiest of all,
   And the home of the blessed, the fountain of love;

To the church of old Enoch, and of the first-born:
 And gen'ral assembly of ancient renown'd,
Whose names are all kept in the archives of heav'n,
 As chosen and faithful, and fit to be crown'd.

  These are they that are perfect through Jesus' own blood,
   Whose bodies celestial are mention'd by Paul,
  Where the sun is the typical glory thereof,
   And God, and his Christ, are the true judge of all.

Again, I beheld the terrestrial world,
 In the order and glory of Jesus go on;
'Twas not as the church of the first-born of God,
 But shone in its place, as the moon to the sun,

[161]

THE VISION

Behold, these are they that have died without law;
 The heathen of ages that never had hope,
And those of the region and shadow of death,
 The spirits in prison, that light has brought up.

To spirits in prison the Saviour once preach'd,
 And taught them the gospel, with powers afresh;
And then were the living baptiz'd for their dead,
 That they might be judg'd as if men in the flesh.

These are they that are hon'rable men of the earth;
 Who were blinded and dup'd by the cunning of men;
 They receiv'd not the truth of the Saviour at first;
 But did, when they heard it in prison again.

Not valiant for truth, they obtain'd not the crown,
 But are of that glory that's typ'd by the moon:
They are they, that come into the presence of Christ,
 But not to the fulness of God on his throne.

Again, I beheld the telestial, as third,
 The lesser, or starry world, next in its place,
 For the leaven must leaven three measures of meal,
 And every knee bow that is subject to grace.

These are they that receiv'd not the gospel of Christ,
 Or evidence, either, that he ever was;
As the stars are all diff'rent in glory and light,
 So differs the glory of these by the laws.

These are they that deny not the spirit of God,
 But are thrust down to hell, with the devil, for sins,
 As hypocrites, liars, whoremongers and thieves,
 And stay 'till the last resurrection begins.

'Till the Lamb shall have finish'd the work he begun;
 Shall have trodden the winepress in fury alone.
And overcome all by the pow'r of his might:
 He conquers to conquer, and saves all his own.

These are they that receive not a fulness of light,
 From Christ, in eternity's world, where they are,
 The terrestrial sends them the Comforter, though,
 And minist'ring angels, to happify there.

THE DEGREES OF GLORY

And so the telestial is minister'd to,
    By ministers from the terrestrial one,
As terrestrial is, from the celestial throne;
    And the great, greater, greatest, seem's stars, moon, and sun.

    And thus I beheld, in the vision of heav'n,
        The telestial glory, dominion and bliss,
    Surpassing the great understanding of men,—
        Unknown, save reveal'd, in a world vain as this.

And lo! I beheld the terrestrial, too,
    Which excels the telestial in glory and light,
In splendour and knowledge, and wisdom and joy,
    In blessings and graces, dominion and might.

    I beheld the celestial, in glory sublime;
        Which is the most excellent kingdom that is,
    Where God, e'en the Father, in harmony reigns;
        Almighty, supreme, and eternal in bliss.

Where the church of the first-born in union reside,
    And they see as they're seen, and they know as they're known
Being equal in power, dominion and might,
    With a fulness of glory and grace round his throne.

    The glory celestial is one like the sun;
        The glory terrestrial is one like the moon;
    The glory telestial is one like the stars,
        And all harmonize like the parts of a tune.

As the stars are all different in lustre and size,
    So the telestial region is mingled in bliss;
From the least unto greatest, and greatest to least,
    The reward is exactly as promised in this.

    These are they that came out for Apollos and Paul;
        For Cephas and Jesus, in all kinds of hope;
    For Enoch and Moses, and Peter and John;
        For Luther and Calvin, and even the Pope.

For they never received the gospel of Christ
    Nor the prophetic spirit that came from the Lord;
Nor the covenant neither, which Jacob once had;
    They went their own way, and they have their reward.

[163]

THE VISION

By the order of God, last of all, these are they,
    That will not be gather'd with saints here below,
To be caught up to Jesus, and meet in the cloud:
    In darkness they worshipp'd; to darkness they go.

These are they that are sinful, the wicked at large,
    That glutted their passion by meanness or worth;
All liars, adulterers, sorcerers, and proud,
    And suffer as promis'd, God's wrath on the earth.

These are they that must suffer the vengeance of hell,
    'Till Christ shall have trodden all enemies down,
And perfected his work, in the fulness of time,
    And is crowned on his throne with his glorious crown.

The vast multitude of the telestial world—
    As the stars of the skies, or the sands of the sea;
The voice of Jehovah echo'd far and wide,
    Every tongue shall confess and they all bow the knee.

Ev'ry man shall be judg'd by the works of his life,
    And receive a reward in the mansions prepar'd;
For his judgments are just, and his works never end,
    As his prophets and servants have always declar'd

But the great things of God, which he show'd unto me,
    Unlawful to utter, I dare not declare;
They surpass all the wisdom and greatness of men,
    And only are seen, as has Paul where they are.

I will go, I will go, while the secret of life,
    Is blooming in heaven, and blasting in hell;
Is leaving on earth, and a-budding in space:
    I will go, I will go, with you, brother, farewell.

Nauvoo, February, 1843

INDEX

INDEX BY AUTHORITIES